# THE STRAIGHT FURROW

## VIVIENNE DRAPER

*By the author of* The Children of Dunseverick

D1514165

## BRANDON

First published in 1996 by
Brandon Book Publishers Ltd,
Dingle, Co. Kerry, Ireland.

British Library Cataloguing in Publication Data is
available for this book.

ISBN 0 86322 224 2

Typeset by Brandon
Cover design by the Public Communications Centre
Cover painting: *The Harrow* by Walter Frederick
Osborne, RHA (1859-1903), courtesy of the Gorry
Gallery, Dublin
Drawings by Vivienne Draper
Printed by ColourBooks Ltd, Dublin

For my parents
and Ernest

# Contents

# Poor Jesus in the Rain

T HE DAY WE left Dunseverick in County Antrim
to journey to Ardglass in County Down, where
our father was to be the new rector, was the
wettest we had ever experienced, even as used as we
were to extremes of rain and wind on that northern
coast all winter. The rain poured down on our furniture as the big van was being loaded. I stood watching, wondering how everything would fit in: the
tallboy, the dining room table with its claw feet, the
green padded chairs with somebody's monogram in
gold embroidered on the backs which were Father's
latest auction buy. Lila, our live-in maid who was
coming with us to Ardglass for a month or two to
help us settle in, was helping Father, two men from
the parish and the driver to load up the furniture
van. Mother, not long over a bout of rheumatic fever,
directed where things were to go and labelled them
for the different rooms in the new rectory. Father
told her he didn't know what he would do without
her.

When all our things had been neatly stored in the
van, Father arranged with the driver that he would
go on ahead in the car. The big Hillman was soon full
of Father's livestock, with only two seats free for us
children. Two hens, his favourite Rhode Island Reds,
sat uneasily in a wire cage in the boot. He had sold

9

all the other hens but intended to start again with
these two and with the aid of an arrangement he had
negotiated with a poultry farmer in Dunsford, near
Ardglass. In another cage, a small goat peered about
rather fearfully, while Malachi our cat sulked in a cat
box. These four shared the capacious boot of the car,
where father had arranged a large canister of water
to see them all through the long journey. Robert and
Philippa travelled in the car with our dog, an ex-
citable spaniel called Jilly, Robert clutching his
matchbox menagerie of slugs, beetles and other in-
sects, and a hedgehog in a box as well.

When all was ready for the journey, Father toured
the empty house to see that we hadn't left anything
behind. Mother and Helen and I, Lila and Jenny, the
youngest of the five of us, all squeezed into the cab
of the van with the driver. We watched as Father
locked the door of Dunseverick rectory and handed
the key to his erstwhile church warden. They shook
hands solemnly and Father turned quickly to the
car. As he drove off down the avenue between the
tall pines and laburnum trees and we followed, the
rain continued inexorably to fall down like ramrods.
The daffodils, under the weight of the deluge, laid
their heads on the ground as if in sad farewell.

Father had told us not to look back, but, in spite of
my fear of the fate of Lot's wife, I did. The house
looked so lonely, its windows blank, its chimneys
dead. Knowing that another clergyman would come
to live in it, perhaps with other children and their
mother, I felt that I hated them all. Squashed in the
cab with Mother and Helen, and Lila with Jenny on

her knee, I was pressed up against the cab window and my tears ran unnoticed on the wet window pane. Then we breasted a hill, slid down the other side to the Causeway crossroads, and the house was gone, out of sight.

The driver, sensing the gloom amongst us in the cab, began to sing. But when he sang "The Blue Hills of Antrim" in a beautiful haunting tenor voice, it seemed to encourage more tears rather than dispel our sadness. Mother told him he sang so well that he ought to be in a choir, and he answered happily that he belonged to the Ormiston Choir in Belfast. Looking at us, he remarked, "I'd better sing something to make yez smile a bit, or this journey'll be twice as long as it's goin' to be."

He launched into "Kitty of Coleraine" with great panache, but when he saw that we were regarding him wanly, he changed to "When Irish Eyes are Smiling", as if to challenge us into cheerfulness. Mother did manage a smile – being musical, she enjoyed the singing – but the rest of us were still sunk in gloom.

We stopped along the way near Ballymena and Mother produced a picnic lunch. Father, Philippa and Robert came to join us in the van amongst the furniture, Philippa and Robert complaining loudly about the smell in the car. The dog, it seemed, had been sick and the two hens had been fighting with each other during the entire journey so far. Father fed the hens some oats and water and they quietened. He let Jilly out for a run.

Ahead of us the empty road ran through the leaning trees of the Frosses, where bog cotton grew on either side, white and shining in the rain. Attending to the demands of nature, we traipsed through long, wet grass to find convenient hedges or bushes. When I got stung with vicious young nettles, my soreness was etched with rage as I searched for "dockin" leaves to ease the sting.

Jilly, the dog, enjoying her freedom, had disappeared up the fields and it was ages before we found her and got started again. Studying our glum faces, the driver declared solemnly, "I see I'll have to sing a better song," and when we were on the road again he launched into "The Lass of the County Down" and "The Mountains of Mourne".

"There now," he called, "won't that just suit yez all a treat."

Near Belfast we passed a big chapel, outside of which hung a huge crucifix, the body of Christ shining white, wet with rain, its arms outstretched. Jenny, sitting on Lila's knee, half asleep, sat up and took her thumb out of her mouth to exclaim, "Look, poor Jesus in the rain!"

On we went between dripping hedges and flooded roads, splashing through a dull, grey Belfast over square sets that rattled all the furniture in the van and shook us to bits. We passed soaking wet horses pulling drays loaded with bags of coal, their heads lowered, their gait dogged.

"Can we go to Woolworth's?" I cried, remembering Christmas visits to a bright cheerful store.

"Not today," Mother replied. "We have to get on to Ardglass. The driver then has to get back to Belfast with the van. Daddy will take you to Woolworth's another day. Belfast isn't as far from Ardglass as it was from Dunseverick."

As we drew nearer to Downpatrick, the downpour of rain began to lessen and a mist arose, through which we were soon able to make out the bulk of the cathedral ahead.

"This is where you will go to school," Mother said. "Look – there, on the hill."

A large white building loomed through the mist.

"It was a jail once," the driver informed us. "The old entrance is there and an underground passage that led to the courthouse. The prisoners were taken through to have their sentences passed."

I shivered at the prospect of attending school in such grim surroundings. "Will there be cells?" I asked fearfully.

The driver laughed and hastened to reassured me.

"It's a grand modern building now, big classrooms, no cells!"

We drove on through soft, rounded countryside, wet green and misty blue, and suddenly we saw the sea.

"The sea, the sea!" we cried in delight. "Is it our sea, our sea of Moyle?"

"No, no," Mother explained, "we are much further down the coast. This is the Irish sea."

We passed the village of Killough, its long wide street lined with trees in full leaf. There we could see a wide bay and across it we could make out what Mother said was Ardglass. Father had told us to look out for a monkey puzzle tree below a tower on a hill,

*The Mournes*

and we could see the tower now. Ardglass, we had learned, meant "the green height", and we could see how it had got its name. On the other side of the bay lay Coney Island, a row of cottages and bigger houses around a bit of seaweed strewn strand. Then as we climbed a hill, the monkey puzzle came into our view, standing very tall with waving arms; it was indeed a veritable landmark.

"It's in the rectory garden," Mother said, smiling. "We'll not get lost: it can be seen for miles."

And there was our new home. We turned in at wide iron gates between stone pillars on to a gravel sweep before a long, low, ivy-covered house. There was no avenue, but we could immediately see what looked like an interesting garden boasting a wooden pergola laced with climbing rose plants.

"Lovely in the summer," Mother commented happily.

A crazy-paved path through the pergola led to a high ivy hedge with a little arch in it leading to another garden beyond, where the monkey puzzle grew. We began to look forward to exploring our new surroundings, but first we had to help get the animals into their quarters. Father brought us to a large square yard at the back of the house with outhouses all around it.

"One for the hens," Father directed. "This one for the goat," indicating a large one. "I'll be getting another goat. There's one will do for the dog. And there's an outside WC. Now that's handy. It's a flush one too."

Outside the yard was a haggard where Father

intended to tether his goats. Alongside the rectory ran a big field which was let to a farmer whose sheep and cows grazed quietly, not bothering each other. The cows came to see who we were, gazing at each of us in turn with big solemn eyes.

Then we were called in. Mother was very tired after the long journey, and a lady from the parish came to take us to tea in the nearby King's Castle. We were thrilled: tea in a castle! It was explained that it was run by the Co-operative movement as a restaurant and hotel. Father stayed with some men who had arrived to help their new rector get the furniture into the rectory, and Lila stayed to make tea for them all. A huge box of groceries which had arrived from the local grocery "with compliments" was deposited in the glass porch.

We longed to explore the house but were equally eager to see the castle, which we soon discovered to be a splendid place with ivy-covered walls, a stone porch and a big entrance into a hall of dark wood where a huge log fire burned in a marble fireplace. From the windows there was a wonderful view over the harbour and out to sea. There were no other guests, and we were ushered into a big red and gold room with another blazing log fire. Mother sank thankfully on to a red velvet couch and we all gathered around her. The lady, Miss Hanna, ordered boiled eggs and toast and a pot of tea, and a small table was brought so that we could stay by the fire. We relaxed and ate our fill as homemade scones and a Victoria sandwich cake completed a most enjoyable meal. Jenny and Robert fell asleep and Mother observed, "I feel just like that too," so Miss Hanna took us back to the rectory and we thanked her profusely.

We older girls were far too excited for early bed and set out on a tour of our new home. A glass porch stood before the front door, inside which was a hall with two beautiful semi-circular mahogany steps leading to the dining room and the stairs. Another room, with a door into the garage, led off the dining room, and this Father quickly claimed as his study. On the right of the hall, the drawing room had a distinctive horse-shoe shaped brick fireplace. All the front windows featured a great many small square panes of glass: "Hard to clean," commented Mother, but we thought them charming, like the windows in the illustrations in our Charles Dickens books. A long stone passage led from the hall to the kitchen, where a row of bells hung.

"For summoning the servants to the dining room and drawing room," Father explained; "there must be bell-pulls in them."

"It's no wonder they were needed," Mother said; "it's a long way from the dining room. The food would be cold surely carrying it up that long passage."

"I'm sure they're not working anyway, and we'll have to think of something better. Lila wouldn't like us rattling bells at her."

We went upstairs. At the first turn of the stairs, watery evening sunlight shone through a lovely stained-glass window and warm colours flowed over the sill and on to the bare boards and landing. There were four bedrooms at the front of the house, and I quickly decided that I loved a little one over the porch, which gave a view over the garden and beyond.

"Oh, please, please, a room of my own, please, Daddy!" I pleaded.

"We'll see, we'll see; let's get your Mother comfortable first, and these sleeping children."

Father carried Jenny and Robert into a bedroom off Mother's room and Philippa and Helen shared another. Father went along a long corridor to a room where he would sleep. It overlooked the field beside the house and in the morning he would be wakened by the cows rubbing themselves against the wall just under his window. Away beyond that the Mourne Mountains were to be seen, which pleased him greatly.

"There's a branch of a tree in the way of my complete view," he reported. "It'll have to come down."

He had been a great man for a view always, and in Dunseverick he'd had a window put into the old loft over the coach house.

There was a little room near the bathroom for Lila, which had a tiny fireplace in it.

"I'm going to light it immediately," she reported. "I'm frozen and stiff with all the goings-on today."

"Well, we're settled for now," Father said with a yawn, and suddenly looked at me.

"You can have the little room," he announced, and a split second later he nearly overbalanced from the flying hug I gave him.

I raced for my room and looked out of the window.

It overlooked the garden, then an expanse of fields and valleys, shadowy now in the fading light. The village of Killough lay beyond, and St John's point. And far away over it all loomed the dark blue shapes of the Mountains of Mourne.

"Oh, it's gorgeous," I breathed, "the Delectable Mountains again." I had always loved *The Pilgrim's Progress*.

I went to Mother's room and found her lying exhausted on the bed Lila had made up for her.

"Fend for yourselves tonight," she said. "I'll be better in the morning."

"I've got the dearest wee room." I glowed with happiness.

"Well, you're the eldest. See that you keep it tidy," admonished Mother.

Nothing could diminish my pleasure in having a room of my own.

"If I don't think of Dunseverick," I reasoned to myself, "I know I'll be happy here."

I undressed and got into bed, leaving my curtains open, my door shut, secure in my own space at last.

*The Delectable Mountains*

# No Laughing Matter

WE HAD NOT been long in Ardglass when Mother decided that our North Antrim accents were too broad and we'd have to have elocution lessons. I balked at this, especially when our elocution teacher made us read poetry in an accent she didn't even use herself.

"She's trying to make us speak with English accents," I cried indignantly, "but we're not English!"

So insistent were my objections that happily the lessons were dropped.

"The accent will fade," Father reasoned with Mother, "in no time at all, when they get to school."

The transition from country to town posed other problems. In Dunseverick we had had few other children to mix with and had relied mainly on ourselves. We were painfully shy. Now in Ardglass we drew back from other children, or stood and stared.

"Don't gawk!" Mother pleaded.

"You're an awful pack of gawms!" Father exclaimed.

But soon Robert and Jenny were going to a one-teacher school next door where a very nice lady took them in charge, and the difference in them was amazing. They came and went by themselves, learned their lessons happily, and took to running in at lunchtime and tell Mother all about it.

Philippa, Helen and I were to attend Down High School in Downpatrick.

Father had been to see the headmaster, and as he had been a teacher before he went into the church, they understood each other. But even before joining the school we had heard he was a very strict headmaster and we were already frightened of him. He taught Latin and was known to expel pupils who were caught behaving badly in school uniform, cheating in exams, or damaging school or other property. Consequently he had a very orderly school with good examination results; it was a greatly respected establishment amongst the farming community in that part of County Down, boys and girls coming from as far as Saintfield, Ballynahinch and Crossgar to be educated. I began to be extremely nervous about the prospects of entering this so admired institute of learning. Was there never going to be any fun?

"You don't attend school to have fun!" roared Father.

Father brought us to school dressed in our smart new green uniforms, "Floreat Dunum" emblazoned in gold on the blazer pocket. He took us in the car at first, but soon we insisted on going on the train with other children from Ardglass whom we had got to know. Others joined the train at halts and stations along the line, and among these were Catholic children going to the "Red High" in Downpatrick. The division between Catholic "Red High" and Protestant "Green High" marked a childhood boundary, a taking of sides, which easily took on the character of a division between "sworn enemies", making the short railway journey exciting in its way. The boys leaned perilously far out of the carriage windows calling each other names, and for the first time I heard the words "Fenian" and "Taig", and the more friendly "Mickey", answered by "Prod" and "Proddy Snobby". But for all its shrillness, the sparring that went on didn't seem to be all that serious, and there were frequent calls of "See you on the half eight" and "See you down the harbour" from both camps.

Some time after we had got to know some of the local Catholic children, a rumour ran through Ardglass that the statue of the Virgin Mary in the grotto in front of the chapel was weeping. We joined the children along the railings, eager to see the miracle. What a pretty sad face she had, I thought, and sure enough the face was wet. However, just then Father came driving past and, seeing us, stopped the car abruptly. He got out and opened the car doors.

"Get in!" he ordered. "Get in you pack of eejits!" He drove us smartly home.

"There they were," he complained to Mother, "standing gawking at the stone statue with a bunch of wee Mickeys in front of the chapel ..."

"But, Daddy," we protested, "her face was shining wet with tears."

"Balderdash!" exploded Father. "It's been raining, there's a hole in the roof of the grotto ..."

"Come here, children." Mother's voice was soft and reasonable. "You must be careful of other people's religion. They might be hurt and offended at you all staring at their statue ..."

"But, Mammy," I still protested, "she has a sad face. Why wouldn't she be weeping to lose her son?"

"Oh, indeed she had reason for tears," Mother said, her arm around Robert, "but just don't be going there out of curiosity. It wouldn't be nice. Just walk past quietly, respectfully."

We promised. It was our first lesson in observing the difference.

We loved travelling to and from school on the train, but one day on the afternoon train home a boy tried to get into our railway carriage, although the boys and girls always travelled in separate carriages. An older boy from our school, he went by the nickname of "Feeler", and the reason why the girls avoided him was obvious enough, apart from the fact that he was fat and pimply and had a close-shaven red head.

Leaving his carriage with the boys, who cheered him on, he crawled along the side of the train from carriage to carriage until he appeared at our window leering in at us, undeterred by the fact that the train was rattling along at a good speed. The window in the door was down, the strap hanging. Swift as lightning, a girl called Debbie Clark jumped to it and, grabbing the strap, pulled with all her might and the window shot up, dislodging Feeler just as he reached the door. The train was now crossing Munce's Lake, and there was a loud splash as Feeler hit the water.

As a new girl I had been keeping out of the "goings on", leaving it to the others, but now I was alarmed. Feeling that the boy would surely be drowned, I

24

reached for the communication cord and the train pulled to a reluctant halt.

The guard came along the side of the track shouting angrily at the carriages.

"Which of youse young hooligans pulled it this time? I'll have the polis on to you as sure as me name's Fred."

The driver left his cab and joined him.

"Grammar school indeed! It's Borstal youse should all be in, and it's where youse'll all be ending up. There's me dinner'll be spoiled again. What is it this time?"

"Joe Peden's in the lake. He was climbing along the train," Debbie explained, "trying to get into our carriage, frightening the wee ones." She put her arm round a small trembling girl. I felt very shaken too.

Just then we heard a shout, and a boat came along beside the train. In it sat a wet, bedraggled Feeler and a man who turned out to be his father, who happened to be fishing in the lake at the very time Feeler had taken the plunge.

There was a great deal of shouting, Joe's father threatening to sue the Belfast and County Down Railway.

The driver was disgusted. "Sue who you like. I'm off home for my dinner."

With that he returned to his cab, the shouting petered out and the train started down the track again.

The guard stayed in our carriage, "eliciting the truth" he said, and looked at me.

"What's your father going to say about this? And

the headmaster?" He was almost gleeful. I was in tears.

"I thought he'd be drowned," I cried.

Debbie stood up for me. "She's only new, and it's the boys cause all the trouble on the train, not us."

She put her arm around her small sister who was crying too.

"Wouldn't be surprised if you aren't all suspended," the guard continued. "And I could refuse to let you travel on the train."

Debbie was ready for him. "Why bully us?" she cried. "Go and read your riot act to the boys. I'm going to tell my father the whole story."

Knowing that her father was a magistrate who sat on the bench in Downpatrick, the guard suddenly changed his tune. "Okay, okay, just a warning. I'll see that the boys get one too."

I was still shaken when we disembarked at Ardglass, the end of the line.

"Don't worry, Viv," Debbie called, "I'll tell your Dad the truth. But next time just you let Feeler drown."

We were hauled before the headmaster. My father had heard my side of the story, which was soon all over Ardglass, and he looked stern but also said not to worry. It seemed Joe Peden's father was carrying out his threat to sue the railway, but also proposed to sue the school.

In the headmaster's office the atmosphere was unnerving, and I was shaking. The head and Father looked calm, and then Debbie came in with her father, who looked at me sternly at first and then suddenly winked. But I still shook. Would I be sent to jail, I wondered; placed on remand maybe? We were waiting for Mr Peden and Joe. I wished they'd hurry up. I wanted this awful situation to be over. I'd left my mother crying at home. It was so unjust. Was I to be punished for saving a fellow's life? Then they appeared, Feeler looking sheepish, constantly blowing a red nose into a grubby handkerchief.

"Let us proceed," said the headmaster. "Mr Clark, will you take over please?"

The magistrate took the head's vacated chair.

"Now, Mr Peden," he said, "I have heard the defence in this case. My daughter has told me the whole story. Now you tell me your side of it."

He folded his arms.

Mr Peden began. "There was me doing a quiet bit of fishing in the lake when there was this almighty splash and a lot of squealing and shouting on the train. I rowed as fast as I could, and there was my own son soaked to the skin. Near drowned he was ..."

My father intervened. "I fish there too, and the water near the railway crossing is only three feet deep at the most ..."

"Near drownded, I said," Mr Peden continued belligerently. "Now he's likely to get pneumonia!" He pronounced it "pewmonia".

"You're sure it's not compensation setting in?" my father suggested in mild tones.

There was silence in the room except for Joe's exaggerated nose blowing.

Suddenly the headmaster asked sternly. "Mr Peden, why do you think your son's nickname amongst the girls is Feeler?"

Mr Peden looked as though he had been dealt a punch. His head went back. He looked at his son.

"Feeler? Feeler is it? You been interfering with little girls, Joe...?"

He suddenly hit Joe a clout over the head that made the stout boy reel. When he went to grab him by the ear, Joe ran, out of the office and down the hall, out the front door and down the long path to the entrance, his father after him. The big windows of the head's office afforded a clear view of their flight. A solemn silence reigned for a few minutes, then a roar of laughter dispersed the tension. But I didn't find it funny. I had nearly been the subject of a great injustice, and that was no laughing matter to me.

# Sunshine and Shadow

ARDGLASS WAS PRINCIPALLY a fishing port, and a few shopkeepers made a good living supplying all the local needs. In the hinterland were farmers, big and small, who gathered in Downpatrick on Fair Days, bringing their livestock and transforming the streets and pavements there into extended farmyards.

In the middle of Ardglass stood the Church of Ireland church of St Nicholas, a grey stone building with a tall spire, which had been built in 1813 by the Board of First Fruits, a name that intrigued us, our young imaginations summoning up all kinds of wonderful images of cornucopias and the like. In the entrance porch, a headstone dated 1585 had been set into the wall. Inside, long pews of dark wood stood in rows, many of them claimed as their own by particular parishioners, especially the members of the local gentry; although rents for pews, which had been a feature of olden days, were no longer collected, people would not dream of trespassing by sitting in anyone else's pew. The Church of Ireland population of Ardglass amounted to about sixty families – definitely a minority; there was a thriving Presbyterian church, but the majority were Roman Catholic. Members of the three denominations lived together amicably, passing the time of day and respecting each other's differences.

Father's second parish, Dunsford, was even smaller than Ardglass. A farming community, it had a small, barn-shaped stone church with a bell on its slate roof which was rung by the sexton at noon every Sunday. Father took the Ardglass service at 10.30 in the morning, had it over by 11.30, dashed home for a cup of tea and a snack, and left in time to get to Dunsford for 12.00 o'clock. We often went with him, and Mother too when she was able, and the people there seemed to like to see us in their front pew regularly, though for us two services one after another sometimes proved too much. In the end Father agreed that we could go to either, as long as at least one of us accompanied him to Dunsford.

He was very proud of his family and often put us all into the car to go with him on parochial visiting. We enjoyed our outings in the country. At one farm we had great fun sliding up and down hayricks with the farm children. They were a happy, healthy little bunch – nine of them. "And another on the way," their parents said, grinning sheepishly.

"Blessed is the man that hath his quiver full," quoted Father genially, which brought forth a loud guffaw from the man and a wry look from his wife, big in her pregnancy. Father introduced us, something he always relished. First he brought me forward, then made the others stand in a row.

"This is Vivien, the eldest."

I was still the tallest then, for it was not until I reached fourteen that I stopped growing and had to look on resentfully at Philippa growing steadily

30

*Country leisure*

taller and then passing me out.

"This is Philippa."

Both of us had short brown hair cut straight around our heads, half way up our ears and in a fringe across our foreheads.

"Next, Helen."

She was fair, with curls, and pretty. We glowered as she smiled sweetly.

Then Robert was brought forward, a small dark-eyed boy.

"This is my son," announced Father rather solemnly. Then, after a pause, "And last, the baby: Jenny."

"I'm not a baby!" she protested vigorously. Fair with grey-green eyes and a wide, usually smiling mouth, she was four years old; she was scowling now.

"Five childer," exclaimed the man; "sure you're only half way!"

"That's my quota," retorted Father. "The wife's not well."

As we followed Father back to the car, I saw the woman suddenly face her husband and declare belligerently, "Now there goes a decent man!"

Mother became unable to walk much, but she liked to go visiting with Father and to accompany him to church in the car, though she was terrified by the way he drove.

"Far too fast, on these narrow roads," she complained. "What if we meet a herd of cows or a flock of sheep?"

And often they did, Father stopping to have a chat with the herdsman or shepherd while the animals strayed all over the road and into the wrong fields; there was hell to pay, as it was described, getting them all together again.

Geese, not frightened by cars or by anybody, their strong hard beaks eager to nip or even take a bite where they could, constituted another hazard of the roads: We were scared of the gaggles of them that wandered where they willed. We loved ducks, their ducklings and the goslings, which Jenny confused and called "ducklets", and we watched them avidly as they plopped about in ponds and rivulets.

Mother ran the house with Lila's help, seeing to regular meals, which were cooked on the big kitchen range or on a double burner primus stove in summer, when it was too hot to light the range except at weekends for hot water for baths.

Mother still played the piano, and sometimes the organ in church, but her hands gradually became stiff and painful. The rheumatoid arthritis from which she suffered was progressive, and with great sadness, for she loved both the organ and the piano, she had to give up. Her talent passed me by but emerged in Philippa and, later, in Jenny.

We all went to music lessons with a Miss Bird who lived in Castle Place, who had a strange method of teaching. She showed us the inside of the piano and told us to note the movement of the little pegs as she played the keys. We had to clench our fingers and then shoot them out smartly on to the notes in time to a metronome, imitating the way in which the pegs shot in and out. It was very difficult to accomplish and our fingers became quite sore, especially as Miss Bird was inclined to rap them with a hard little stick, much a a jockey urges his horse on with a riding whip. We complained at home as we had done about the elocution lessons, and after a while the piano lessons were stopped. Mother taught us herself then for as long as she could, but I certainly showed no signs of becoming a concert pianist, later finding myself still at the "Primrose Waltz" stage when I reached the age of seventeen. Philippa and Jenny, however, played both organ and piano very competently.

One memorable summer afternoon Philippa was playing "L'Après-Midi d'une Faun" on the piano in the drawing room, Mother and I listening, the window open, when a bird joined in from the shrubbery. Philippa played a bar, then waited, and the bird repeated the notes. We listened intently and Philippa played the same bar again and the bird answered. The experience was uncanny and mystical, a never-to-be-forgotten "après-midi".

Father was a popular and charismatic figure, genial and kindly, and he generally got on well with everybody of all classes.

"He has a way with him," people often said. Until, that is, he fell foul of the County Down staghounds.

First he had sympathised with a parishioner who had suffered a broken fence and a gate left open in an onrush of horses and hounds over his land, and who had been left with no apology.

"Very arrogant," Father pronounced.

Then, one quiet afternoon Mother was sitting in her chair in the shrubbery when, with a great thudding of hooves, the hunt came galloping down the field next to the rectory, over our garden wall on to the gravel, some of them straying over the lawn and perilously near Mother, and out of the gate which was always open, hallooing and hurrahing like dervishes.

Purple with fury, Father immediately jumped in the car and drove to where he knew the hunt habitually ended. There he confronted the master of hounds, and he had no intention of mincing his words.

"You could have killed my wife!"

The man, resplendent in his pink coat, did not dismount. Keeping the advantage of height, he looked down haughtily at my apoplectic father.

"My good man..." he began, and tapped my father on the shoulder with his riding whip.

Father grabbed the whip and roared: "Get down off that horse, you blackguard, you! I'll not hurt the beast, but you! I'll use this to horsewhip you black and blue! Invading private property! Frightening helpless women! And you dare to address me as your good man!"

A young huntsman rode between the two. Father recognised him as the son of one of his farmer parishioners from the Dunsford countryside.

"I'll apologise. What some of us did was unpardonable. I hope your wife is all right." Dismounting, he held out his hand.

Mollified, my father nodded slowly, his anger dissipating as he accepted the apology.

"A nice lad that," he said as he related the incident to Mother later. "A son of the land and a gentleman. The others don't come up to his shoulders, even though their egos are as big as their arses."

"Don't be rude," Mother reproved him, as she turned away to disguise her smile.

# First Parting

ARDGLASS SOON REVEALED itself to be a lively little place. Its two harbours were full of boats, and when the herring season was at its height, the boats lay so close to each other that the fishermen could walk from one harbour to the other across them. Girls from Scotland – "gutter girls" they were called – came to gut the fish, standing at long tables on the harbour, their fingers silver with fish scales and often bandaged, so sharp were the knives they used. Father took us to the harbour at night to see them under lights erected so that they could go on working to fill the herring boxes, the fish flying fast through their nimble fingers. As he later described it, the scene was rich and mediaeval, the sea on a rough night roaring over the harbour wall and drenching the women.

We thought Ardglass a real metropolis after the quiet spaces of Dunseverick. There were several shops, two hotels besides King's Castle, two public houses, an ice-cream shop and at least two sweet shops. With so much to chose from, we discovered an urgent need for more pocket money. Mother said that we'd all have to get ourselves jobs! Everyone in the town seemed jolly and a good living was made by many in Ardglass; the shops thrived, as did the local boarding houses and the two hotels.

*Boats in harbour at Ardglass*

Father had soon arrived at an arrangement with a fisherman. He would have a dozen herring on a string and, as Father drove past on the harbour, he'd throw these with unerring aim through the open passenger window of the car, where they'd land on the seat or in the lap of one of us. As the resulting smell of fish couldn't be got rid of, we were teased in school by our fellows, who sniffed derisively, and finally we refused to drive in the car at all.

Father became a dab hand at cooking the herring himself, filleting them for frying or potting them in vinegar, and very good eating they were.

There were other good reasons for avoiding the car, all of which had to do with Father. Father had earned with some ease the reputation of being a "tarrible" driver, given to scattering hens, geese and all manner of livestock, which were used to having the roads to themselves. Once he ran over a chicken and bargained with the poultry farmer for it, bringing it home for us to cook. With good reason we decided we preferred our bicycles for transport, and we took to riding out into the countryside for buttermilk or eggs, country butter and home-baked bread.

Each of us had a bit of the garden to attend to, and Father dug and planted potatoes and cabbages, rows of peas and beans, just as he had done in Dunseverick. He wore an ancient pair of trousers for gardening which he referred to as his "moleskins", in deference to one of his favourite authors, Sean O'Casey.

Mention of Dunseverick was banned for a time because we had bouts of homesickness. We tried to recapture the fun we had had in that far away place we loved and we tried to play the same games, but the savour had gone.

"You are growing up, that's all," Father said. "This is a new phase."

Mother wasn't well and the local doctor shook his head. "Just keep going," he said and prescribed gold treatment. We were intrigued.

"You'll become very valuable, Mother," I said precociously. "We'll get a good price for you."

Everyone laughed, but Father assured her that she was very valuable even without the gold. She was indeed. She still ran the house from her bed or chair, always knew where everything was, chivvied Father and us, ordered the groceries and was charming to visitors.

But the treatment sadly didn't do any good. That first year in Ardglass, she was able to walk down the hill to church with us; then she needed a stick. Then came the time when Father, puffing and blowing, having put on a lot of weight, had to carry her upstairs to bed each night. Finally she had to use a wheelchair, which was a great big, long, cumbersome thing, like a Victorian bath chair, which Father had got as a bargain from the family of a deceased parishioner. Mother moved down to his study off the dining room, where the door into the garage proved useful for the unwieldy invalid chair, for our beautiful, lively mother was now an invalid, some said a cripple. She was terribly thin and pale and always cold. Father went to Downpatrick and, without any of his usual bargaining, bought her a leather coat.

"That'll keep the cold out," he said gently as he helped her to put it on. She loved it, of course, and with all the cushions and rugs we heaped on her, she all but disappeared into the wheelchair. Then we wheeled her out through the garage into the garden, which she loved, where we parked her under an orange-blossom tree, the silky white petals falling on her. She liked to have her tea out there, and all was well until we had to replace Lila. She had not returned to the north after all, but had married an Ardglass man and gone to live in a nice little house on the Bray. We would have to find someone who would look after Mother for us while we were at school.

Father made the bedroom he used at the end of the long passage into a study and Robert was given Lila's little room beside the bathroom. Father took over what had been Mother's bedroom, and because his snoring penetrated into the room off it where Philippa and Helen slept, Philippa went into the guest room, leaving Helen and Jenny to put up with the sonorous sound. All these changes made me nervous and I hung grimly on to my little room over the porch.

Father eventually found a nice local girl to come and help in the house and take care of Mother. Mary Magee was Catholic, and we loved to ask her about saints, rosaries, the confessional and what the priest said to her when she admitted to sinning, what penance he gave.

"Surely you haven't a sin to confess every time you go to chapel!" we exclaimed. "You're such a good person."

41

She laughed, "You'd be surprised when you examine your conscience how many sins you commit."

Mary had a boyfriend and went for walks with him over the golf links in the evenings and on her days off. One hot sunny day we followed them at a safe distance and peered over a rock to where they had found a sheltered spot. Several pairs of curious eyes watched them cuddle and kiss, but when Mary removed her blouse and the boyfriend began to rub her back and shoulders with sun-tan oil, we looked at each other, feeling suddenly guilty, and crept silently away. They eventually got married and went to live in a pretty house overlooking the Protestant graveyard.

But while she was with us, Mary was good and kind with Mother, making her dainty meals and bringing her flowers, sympathising with her pain and saying prayers for her in chapel. She also did her best to keep the house clean and tidy, but it was big and rambling, and she had enough to do seeing to the range in the kitchen, cooking and washing, ironing and cleaning all the little window panes.

When we came home from school, Mary went home and we made the evening meals, taking it in turn. Philippa and Helen took domestic economy in school, where there was an excellent teacher, and they often brought home delicious examples to share, from savoury dishes to cakes. Having opted for science and possessing neither aptitude nor training in the culinary arts, I was always glad of Father's potted herrings or boiled eggs when it came my turn to make the meal. Robert was excused housework, but he enjoyed the male privilege of doing outside jobs with Father, cleaning out the livestock's quarters, collecting eggs and tethering the goats in the haggard each day. Father had acquired another goat, a billy goat; referred to as "the bucker" because it packed a lethal punch, it was a dreadful creature which stank to high heaven. For some strange reason Robert was able to handle it, and it seemed to like him. We asked why and Father said Robert must be related to it, which caused us, of course, to yell with laughter and call him "the bucker's cousin", and this drove Robert as mad as the goat himself. We teased Robert so much that it led to Father having a serious conversation with Mother.

"He'll have to go to boarding school. It's not good for him to be with females all the time."

"But he's so young," Mother pleaded, "only a little boy. There are other wee boys at the elementary school. Sure he's happy there. Wait a bit ... when he's older."

Her pleas were in vain, however, and Robert was packed off at the age of eight to Cabin Hill, the preparatory school for Campbell College in Belfast. I felt guilty.

"We shouldn't have teased him so much," I said to Philippa, and we both cried.

"It'll make a man of him," Father assured Mother and us. "I'll take you up at half term to Belfast and you'll see."

But he looked small and vulnerable in his new black- and white-ringed school cap, sitting on his trunk in the porch while Father brought the car round. It was a tearful parting.

"Belfast isn't the moon," Father chided indignantly. "He'll be home in the holidays."

# Early Learning

THERE WERE SOME "grandees", or landed gentry, belonging to the parish, and one day Father was asked to drive a lady of this calibre to Belfast where she was to name a ship ready for launching at the docks. She didn't drive herself and her chauffeur was sick, and despite his reputation as a driver, Father had been chosen by her to be her replacement chauffeur for the day. Before departing she came to lunch at the rectory, and we children had to be on our best behaviour. I was going to the launching too, with Father, and I was curious and excited.

The lady was tall and thin, expensively dressed, and haughty. She wore her hat throughout the meal and only removed her gloves to place them neatly beside her place at the table. There was none of the usual chatter during the meal, the lady addressing her remarks to Father and eating so little Mother looked at her almost untouched plate in consternation.

"Don't worry," I heard Father whisper to Mother later, "she's so polite she'd copulate with her hat on."

At the docks in Belfast, I mounted the platform with Father and the lady and several other dignataries and, standing there and looking around me, was astonished by the beauty of this enormous ship.

45

After a succession of speeches, the moment we had been waiting for arrived and the lady, at the appropriate moment, swung a bottle at the prow of the ship, where it smashed into shining fragments, the contents dribbling down the new paint work. She named it in a Princess Royal voice, *HMS Atlantic*.

I watched all the men who had built the ship standing on her deck and along the quayside, doffing their caps and cheering as she began to slide down to the sea.

"Daddy," I whispered, "why couldn't one of those men name the ship? Do they get to sail in her? They built her."

He shushed me, but one man heard and said laughingly to Father, "You've got an embryo socialist there."

Back in Ardglass we left the lady home, still hatted and gloved and declaring herself exhausted. Later I looked in the dictionary for "copulate". I knew there was no use asking Father. He'd only give me a "quare" answer. The dictionary definition of copulate read "... the act of mating". I'd seen dogs, cats, sheep and cows mating and didn't think much of it, except that I accepted the necessity for the production of little puppies, kittens, lambs and other small furry things. But that lady! I was glad I would probably never meet her again.

When I was eleven I discovered that I had been struck by what was called "the curse". Unprepared for it, I thought I was dying. Mother, however, told me that I was maturing early, which sounded so much more acceptable than dying. So I was surprised that she was alarmed when, at the age of twelve and a half, I began to take an interest in boys.

The first boy to engage my attention was the church organ blower. The bellows for the organ was situated in the vestry and the blower sat in the choir seats. At a given signal he slipped into the vestry and got the bellows going so that the organ could emit sound. As the job had a small remuneration with it, there was no shortage of volunteers. The particular boy I fancied was called Willi, spelt with an "i", and for some reason I thought this a romantic name. I sat where I could stare at him in the choir and connect with his big brown soulful eyes; I found that it was quite easy to get them locked into mine, though when the signal came to get the bellows going, it seemed that he almost ran with relief.

Father saw what was going on and told Mother.

"She's reading too many romantic novels. There she sits ogling that poor silly Willi until he doesn't know whether he's on his head or his feet."

Ogling sounded a horrible word and I was offended, so I decided to demonstrate my self-control by desisting from looking at Willi in church the next Sunday. One service later Willi stayed in the vestry instead of coming out and the organist pressed the organ's keys in vain. Father announced the hymn number again, and again there was silence, apart from the rattle of the keys as the organist frantically pressed them. Father flew across the sanctuary, surplice flying, into the vestry, where he found Willi fast asleep. After an audible scuffle and a few hissed epithets, the clattering and wheezing of the bellows began and the flustered organist produced the music.

After that incident Willi lost my attention; a fellow who couldn't fulfil such a simple but important function held no allure for me. Subsequently the church gathered up the funds for an electric organ and organ blowers became redundant.

Another boy soon caught my attention on the train to and from school. Tall and fair and shy, he was called Tom and he was Catholic. He joined the train at a halt on the way to Downpatrick. It was immediately apparent that he wasn't one of the "hooligans", as the railway guard called the boys that gave trouble on the train, and whenever I passed his carriage, he seemed to be reading. It would have been impossibly bold of me to get into his carriage, and I was frustrated by my inability to catch his attention. Sheep's eyes through the carriage window as I slowly passed did no good; he was unaware of my existence. An older girl liked him too. She'd been to the films and said he looked like Alan Ladd and showed me a picture of the film star in a magazine. I begged it from her and, when she cut it out and gave it to me, I stuck it on the mirror in my room. Then I had an idea. I had been reading an A. J. Cronin novel and copied a love letter out of it. Now the only problem was how to get it to Tom on the train. I didn't know his surname, but I knew a girl who boarded the train at the same halt. I gave her the note. But she showed it to my sister, who was in her class in our school, and she was so horrified she took it to Father. I was summoned to the study that evening. Back against the wall, I denied the whole thing. I hadn't signed it except as "your lover". He raged at me, enormously angry.

"Do you know what a lover is?"

I didn't, but wouldn't acknowledge my ignorance.

"What do you think the boy's parents and teachers would suppose if that got around? A Catholic boy! I'd be disgraced. Your mother would be disgraced."

At this I broke down and cried.

That night Father took away my copy of *Tess of the D'Urbervilles* and the offending Cronin. I had only been half way through Tess. Then he had a consultation with Mother. I tried to listen but dared not hang about. I heard enough to remind me of the same consultation they'd had before sending Robert to boarding school, and my heart quaked.

# Friendship

NORAH DORAN TRAVELLED on the train from Ardglass to a girl's convent further up the line, and she and I got talking. A little older than I was, she shared my taste for reading novels. Comparing notes about our respective schools, she was envious of the fact that we had men teachers and boys in the class.

"Them ould nuns know nothin'," she said glumly to me one morning. "I'll likely end up a blooming old nun myself."

"No, you won't," I exclaimed. "You are really pretty. You have such big eyes and boys like long hair like yours. And you have such a fine figure."

Norah glowed and hugged me.

"Listen, Norah," I whispered, "there's a bunch of the boys from school coming to fish off the pier on Saturday. I heard them talking about it. You come with me and you'll soon get off with one of them."

She was rapturous.

"Put on a tight jumper and show off your figure. You've even got a better shape than mine, and that's another thing the boys like besides long hair!"

We shrieked with laughter.

"But my brothers say I'm a big lump," Norah was suddenly anxious.

"Brothers!" I was derisive. "Thank goodness I've

only one and he's away at boarding school."

The two of us paraded down the harbour that Saturday like magazine models.

"Where are you going, all tarted up?" asked one of Norah's brothers. We didn't deign to answer him.

We had no trouble with the boys. Immediately two of them gave up the fishing, "for better sport", they told their disgusted mates.

We went out with the boys again the next day, and after school we'd meet up to go for walks across the golf links that ran around the cliffs or lie on the long shore amongst the tufts of pink thrift and bird's foot trefoil. Norah particularly liked a boy called John.

"I want to marry him when I'm old enough," she said solemnly one day, "and he wants to marry me then too."

"My God, and he's a Prod!" I exclaimed, having only just thought of it.

"That's not what's worrying me." Norah kept her head down.

I looked at her. "Sex. That's it, sex."

She nodded. "I'm afraid."

"Aw gosh, sure it's as common as muck. You can learn all about it for getting married. Even the village idiot can do it."

"I know, but I'm scared. Not of the loving bit. Of having a baby."

I looked at her and suddenly remembered something. "Your sister ... she died ... having a baby, didn't she?"

Norah nodded. "It was when I was ten. Deirdre

was so pretty. She had the baby at home and they both died."

"Maybe if she'd gone to hospital ... they take great care of mothers and babies in hospital."

"Mammy kept her at home, to avoid scandal maybe. The doctor didn't come in time."

Norah was crying. "It was the squeals of her, the awful, awful squeals. I heard it. I woke up and heard it. Oh, it was dreadful."

I put my arms around her. "Just you hush now. It's a long way off and it'll be all right. They won't let you feel a wee bit of a pain in hospital."

But Norah still shook.

"I know where there's a book about it," I whispered. "Mother has a book in her drawer, all about things like that. It has a plain white cover. I'll borrow it for you. It's called *Having a Baby*. It'll tell you all you should know about it."

Norah was comforted at last.

So one day on a quiet part of the shore, we sat on a rock with our feet in the sea and read the book.

"Ohhhhh, I didn't know that!" I was confounded. "And read that ... look ... there! It's well we found out about all this."

"Maybe it's a sin, readin' about it," Norah said apprehensively.

"Sin me foot! Haven't you got to know anyway? Instead of going about like a blind donkey. I know one thing, I'll mind myself from now on."

"But I ... love ... John."

"What's that to do with it? Sure you can love him. Just be careful, not too much kissing. Look here ...

53

read some more ... oh wait, quick, someone's coming. Shove it in your bag."

Norah put it away in her shoulder bag and we joined the boys who had come looking for us.

Next day I went straight home after school and didn't wait for Norah because I had a lot of homework to do.

I was startled when Norah appeared at the dining room window gesticulating frantically.

"The book, oh the book!" she screeched through the glass.

I ran outside.

"What's happened?"

"Oh, Jesus, Mary and Joseph, the priest's got the book!" She was crying hysterically.

"Father McManaway! Oh, holy smoke! How? How did he get it?" I cried.

"It must've fallen out of my bag and me Mum found it. Oh God, he'll be sending for me."

"And what are you in such a state for? Think of me! Me Mum's name is in it. Father McManaway'll tell my father. Oh, holy smoke!"

"I begged Mammy not to tell the priest, but she said I'd been running wild lately and needed discipline."

"Oh, you're all right," I said. "You'll only get a talking to and an old penance. But my father'll flay me alive. He'll be far worse than Father McManaway."

As it transpired, Father McManaway was more annoyed with Norah for putting him in an embarrassing position than for any great sinfulness on her part, so he contented himself with giving her an extra penance.

"That's nothing," I complained glumly. "I'm right in the dog house. There's a confab going on right now about me. It'll be boarding school for sure."

"You'd better take care they don't send you to Borstal," Norah cried. "Oh, Viv, I'm the cause of it, and I don't want you to go. What'll I do without you?"

"There, there, it wasn't your fault," I assured her. "Such a fuss about an old book! Say, Norah, I'm glad we read it first, aren't you?"

But I was well and truly hauled over the coals at home. Even Mother, usually so forbearing, was cross with me. I had disappointed her and this made me sad; I wilted under her disapproval.

"I only wanted to help Norah," I sobbed.

"Maybe, but you must not pretend to know more than you do. It's not nice."

I was bewildered, and subdued, for a time.

# The Nickname

O N A FINE high windy day, I accompanied Father in the car on his visits in his second parish. On the way home, encountering a gang of wee boys flying kites, we stopped to watch. I loved kite flying, and when we were small Father had often made us box kites out of wrapping paper, some of which flew and some of which didn't. The boys were having the same trouble today. Then one kite rose above the rest, a beautiful thing with a bird painted on it. It rose steadily, higher and higher, soaring above all the others.

"Lend's it," a boy called to the owner, who gave him the string. It rose higher still, light and easy. Another boy borrowed it, and again it rose above them all. A scuffle ensued, and a boy grabbed the kite string wound on to a piece of cardboard and ran towards some telephone wires. The owner, swift as the kite, jerked the string from him just in time.

"D'you want to destroy it on me?" he cried angrily. "After me lending it to you! Me father made it for me, and him in a wheelchair all day!"

"I don't believe your Dad was shot by the enemy in a battle at all," the boy shouted. "He was more likely run over by an ould tractor."

"He has the gunshot wounds."

They whispered together.

"He'll make you kites if you like. I'll ask him. Then we could have races," the boy's voice was eager. "He'll show you the bullet holes too, maybe."

"What battle was it?"

"Was it the Boyne one?" They broke into jeering laughter.

"Or maybe he was an ould Shinner!"

"Aye, that's more like, an ould Fenian battle!"

One of the boys reached for the kite and grabbed the tail of paper bows, which came off in his hand.

"It'll not fly now," the kite's owner wailed, tears in his eyes. "Me dad'll be cross, after all the work."

The boys ran up the hill again and let their kites catch the wind. A moon had risen in the summer's evening sky and the forlorn boy stood, shoulders drooped, and watched the kites on the skyline.

Then when the boys tired and some of the lines became tangled, ending up in fisticuffs, they came whooping and yelling down the hill. As they passed their erstwhile companion holding the broken kite, they chorused,

"Yah, you Fenian you ... Fenian ... Fenian!"

Father immediately jumped out of the car, his blood pressure rising, and stood in the way of the onrush of boys, who halted when they saw him.

"I'll Fenian you, you ignoramuses!" he roared at them. "Who're ye calling a Fenian? I'm ashamed of the lot of you – all in my Sunday school too. Come on down to my house and I'll teach you what a Fenian is. Get into the car now."

He squashed the whole five of them into the back of the car. Then he saw the boy with the broken kite.

"Is that the so-called Fenian?" he asked the boys.

They nodded and kept their heads down. They knew his Reverence.

"Come on in, boy," he invited, indicating that there was room in the front beside me.

"What is your name, boy?"

"Rory, Fa... sir." The boy seated himself beside me a little reluctantly. "I'll have to go home soon, sir. Me father'll be waiting on me."

"I'll leave you home, but first come to my house and learn a bit of history. Even if you know it already, it'll do you no harm to hear it again."

He brought them all into his study, and Mother came in with milk and biscuits, then urged seconds on them as though they were in for an ordeal and would need the extra sustenance. Then she poked up the fire. It was chilly, for all it was summer.

Father seated himself in the large horsehair chair he had brought from Dunseverick and opened a book. He switched on a lamp beside him. The rest of the room was in darkness save for the firelight. Philippa came and sat with me.

"The Fenian organisation, conceived as a Brotherhood by one James Stephens, and initially unsuccessful in Ireland, spread amongst the Irish in the United States of America..."

Father read on, and an hour later he stopped. Only the sound of soft, steady breathing could be heard. He lifted the lamp. Every boy was fast asleep.

Mother looked in at the door.

"Sure, it's the fresh air has them sleepy and tired,"

she apologised for them, "running around all evening on the hill."

She caressed the nearest one's head.

"They don't give a damn," Father exclaimed, " not a damn."

He woke them all up without ceremony, and sent the village boys home. Rory he took to his home further afield and Philippa and I went along for the ride.

At the door Father explained to Rory's parents what had happened, and his mother laughed.

"Sure, sticks and stones might break your bones, but names'll never hurt you."

But his father, coming to the door in his wheel-chair, contradicted her, saying sadly, "A nickname is the heaviest stone the devil can throw at a man."

Father explained that he believed in teaching the children history.

"History, all history, is the basis of a decent education," he said.

They agreed and invited him in for a chat.

"I'll call again; I have to get these two home," he said indicating us in the car. "I tried to mend the kite. It's a beauty and not too badly torn."

They thanked him and waved as we drove down their lane towards home. Above, on the skyline, the summer moon climbed the sky and the figures of boys and kites were silhouetted against it.

# The Summer Visitors

MOTHER SAID THAT the summer visitors were fast, that their behaviour got them a reputation. We were intrigued. How did you get a reputation? It sounded exciting. These visitors stayed in summer houses on the nearby Coney Island and around the golf links. Every year they took up residence, played golf and went out in boats; they swam and sun bathed, and they smoked and drank in the pubs and golf club. At night they had bonfires on the sandy shore and played guitars and melodeons, music that reached us and had us longing to be with them. But: "They're too sophisticated, too fast for you," Mother said, and we were discouraged from seeking their company. The locals disapproved of their noisy ways, but were glad enough of the trade they brought to the small businesses around.

Gradually, after spending the summer months hanging around at a distance, we did get to know them. They were young men and girls having fun, and we envied them. As we got older we looked forward to their coming every year, for they dispelled winter gloom and brightened up the place, and our lives. We swam with them, joined them at their bonfires; Philippa learned to smoke, and Helen acquired a boyfriend who had a skull on the handlebars of his bicycle. He said he was hoping to do medicine, but he was also a magician and was

61

always coaxing her to let him practise on her, locking her into handcuffs or boxes, and then forgetting the formula to let her out. Eventually he became a full time magician, and Mother said it was just as well for medicine.

Mother had a friend, a Miss Moran, who lived on Coney Island, and she came to Mother one day to tell her about the latest exploits of the summer visitors. Her niece Rosemary, whom we knew she had brought up from babyhood, was counting on the love of one of the visitors she had met the previous year. Miss Moran was concerned. She herself knew of the infidelities and passing fancies of the holiday makers.

But she also had other worries to contend with. Beside her cottage stood several other cottages, which had been rented at first, then purchased as holiday homes by visitors, who had added to them, modernised them, put in electricity, running water and, latterly, deep sewerage. Miss Moran was worried about the deep sewerage. The visitors had erected a disposal unit just across from her cottage which blocked the view of the point of land with the sea just beyond that she had so enjoyed from her living room window.

One of the summer visitors was a building contractor, who was very rich. To us they all seemed very rich. Having bought the cottages, one by one, they had renovated them out of all recognition, making small concessions to the past in the forms of black three-legged pots full of expensive plants, which they placed outside the front doors, and leaded glass in the porch windows, and maybe a boat in a bottle on an alcove shelf – all bought in some arts and crafts shop. They didn't edge their flower beds with shells and stones from the sea shore as Miss Moran did, and she didn't see the point of draping a coarse fishing net over a white wall unless it was to be used for fishing.

Miss Moran told Mother and me (avid as I was for stories, especially stories of romance) that the contractor who was responsible for the concrete disposal unit was the life and soul of the place at weekends when they all arrived in their cars, visited each other and the local pub, and took spanking new boats out in the bay. And it was the building contractor who originated the idea of inaugurating the new sewage disposal unit with a formal ceremony. Meanwhile, Miss Moran was sure that it was his son who had her niece pale and wan with longing, always looking and waiting till she had the heart aching in you. An attractive young devil, he was attending some university across the water and, Miss Moran opined, he had too much time and money at his disposal. "What would Rosemary have in common with that one?"

The trouble was that Rosemary was just the sort of girl, soft and pliable, that that kind of young man couldn't keep his hands off. Miss Moran shed a few tears as long summer days stretched out.

On the day of the ceremony to celebrate the installation of the sewage disposal unit, Miss Moran thought she would have a fit. It was so daft, she reported to us, spluttering with indignation. There they all were, dressed up in long dresses trailing across the sand, the men in morning dress; flowers everywhere, in button holes, on hats and in their hair. Some of the men even had pink thrift and sea campion stuck in their beards. Led by a band, the procession started at the far end of the line of cottages, and as they marched slowly they sang. From what Miss Moran could hear, the words were not the ones she associated with the familiar tunes she knew. At the concrete unit, chairs had been laid out in a semi-circle facing a seat into which the building contractor sat as master of ceremonies. Miss Moran didn't know whether to go for the police or not when she realised that the ceremonial throne was a shiny, modern WC with a big pink bow tied to its handle.

At the end of the first speech, which mercifully she couldn't hear, there was a burst of clapping and festoons of pink, yellow and blue toilet paper leaped from the ground and draped the concrete block. Suddenly a light aircraft appeared from over the headland, everybody waved and danced up and down and the aircraft vomited more toilet paper over the shore and the crowd.

"Did you ever see anything so clean daft?" Miss Moran asked Rosemary as they stood at the window surveying the scene. Rosemary didn't answer, and when Miss Moran turned to her, she involuntarily grasped the girl; she thought she was going to faint, so distraught did she look. She was staring at the crowd of summer visitors who now seemed to be crowning a queen. The young men lifted a girl, a tall sun-tanned blonde in a skimpy costume, to the top of the sewage unit. Then one of them climbed up and draped her in a toilet roll sash. Miss Morgan put her arms around Rosemary who was gazing out, the palms of her hands flat against the window pane. Miss Moran recognised the figure of the contractor's son standing with the blonde, his arm around her waist, kissing her and holding her. He took a ring from his pocket and put it on her finger, and even from where they stood Miss Moran and Rosemary could see that it glittered.There was a burst of applause, and more singing to celebrate the double event.

When the crowd had finally dispersed to their smart cottages or gone off in their fast cars and boats, Rosemary walked slowly across the sand, passed the new acquisition decorated untidily in tattered paper ribbons, and continued to the point where the sea came surging up a little pebbly shore. There hummocks of pink thrift grew.

"A cushion for your head," he'd said, laying her down on a hummock of thrift. Then he'd gently threaded the pink flowers through her hair to form a garland around her face. And leaning over he'd kissed her, and gone on kissing her. The sky had deepened from summer turquoise to dark blue, the first stars had appeared and time had stopped for Rosemary. The lapping of shore water, the calls of birds going home to bed had all been part of a symphony of simple sounds that for her ever afterwards brought equal suffering and joy.

The summer visitors were in their cottages, the lights blazing and music blaring, when Rosemary returned to an anxious Miss Moran. She laid her head in her aunt's lap and her shoulders shook with sobs. She sobbed as she had done when a little girl, and as Miss Moran stroked the dark hair, her own tears made it wet, and pain, tempered with time, welled up in her too as she remembered other summers and other visitors.

# The Grey House

WE MISSED OUR story teller of Dunseverick days, Jane, who had told us such intriguing stories, part history and part her own vivid imagination – the best sort, we decided. Father was a great story teller too, when he had time from parochial duties, and I vowed to remember his tales and write them all down some day. Now I tackled Mother. She understood how we missed the story telling.

"Tell us about County Wicklow, Mammy, about Poulaphouca, where you lived in Blessington, about the people there – not fairy stories, real stories."

Mother smiled. "Shall I tell you about a real ghost?"

"Please, please!" we chorused.

"Well, let's begin," said Mother as we clustered around her in the drawing room, the horseshoe-shaped fireplace blazing with logs and casting flickering shadows on the walls and ceiling. It was a late afternoon in mid-winter and the bushes outside the window tapped on it intermittently.

"I was always fascinated by a tall, grim, grey house that seemed to be part of its background of steep, jagged cliff at the far end of Wicklow town, near Wicklow Head. I had an aunt and uncle who lived in Wicklow, and I used to go to stay with them in the summer holidays. Local people always called the town 'Wickla'; it was a seaside place, on the mouth of the river Vartry, and lots of visitors came to tour around the Wicklow mountains from there. My aunt and uncle took visitors in for the summer months, and one time a strange man came. He said he wanted to buy the tall grey house. We took him to see it. It was reached only by a long winding overgrown avenue of wind-bent trees, and the sea here always seemed to be in a fury of white foam and waves that dashed against the rocks beneath the house. It had been occupied by an eccentric writer who quite obviously had wanted to get as far off the beaten track as possible. But for many years it had lain empty, the tall dark windows blank, the roof green with damp and the garden overgrown.

"Now, this man, whose name was as strange as he seemed, wanted to buy the house and to devote himself to his writing, as had the previous owner. Mr Gemelli spoke with a foreign accent and he told my aunt and uncle, with whom he had become very friendly, that he wanted to bring his wife to Ireland to live in the grey house. She came from Warsaw, he said, and had been brought up in a convent, where he had met her when he went to take art classes with the older children. She had great talent, and when she was eighteen he asked her to marry him. We were astonished when we heard this, for Mr Gemelli looked to be at least forty years old. So when he went away to bring Marguerite back and the house was being made habitable, we were filled with curiosity.

"Some time later we received news that they would arrive in two days and my mind was filled with excited anticipation. I was even more excited when I learned that they would stay with us on the night of their arrival, to recover from their long journey before moving into the house.

"On their arrival I could not restrain myself from staring at Marguerite. I had been expecting a youngish woman like my aunt, but I scarcely expected a girl who seemed hardly older than I was. And she was exquisitely beautiful: tall and slim, with long dark hair and eyes that seemed to be black but in the light were deep blue. She was very shy and her husband had a fatherly, protective air with her.

"The next morning they left for their new home, but one day about a week later my uncle told me that we would be visiting the Gemelli's that very afternoon. I was dying to see inside that mysterious grey stone house. As we neared it with our little pony and trap, we entered the long, forbidding, dark avenue that led to the house. And then we were there, on the gravel sweep before the house, dwarfed by its immense height. There was a basement, the tops of its dark windows just reaching the light, and then three storeys towering up to tall chimneys on the roof. Although the top windows were still blank and uncurtained and the basement was obviously not in use, the middle two rows of windows had taken on a different look. They were shining and draped in frilly voile curtains with posies of fresh flowers in all of them, giving a doll's house appearance in contrast to the rest. The big front door was freshly painted and the brass knocker shone.

"The Gemellis, both of whom spoke fluent, accented English, made us very welcome, Marguerite serving tea with quiet grace but saying little. My uncle and Mr Gemelli held most of the conversation, talking about books and education and things like that. Marguerite kept looking at me shyly. Then suddenly she smiled, stood up and held out her hand to me. Together we ran outside, and here she took me down, down, in a wild race through the steep terraced garden, to the very edge of the sea. I was quite frightened, feeling that there was something frantic in the way this girl ran when released from that elegant drawing room, dragging me willy-nilly with her, laughing and dancing over the rocky garden paths. Then, as suddenly as she had initiated our flight from the house, she stood still and silent on a rock. Here the waves washed over her shoes, and she let them, unheeded. She still held my hand, and when I protested that I was getting wet, she laughed again and set off on another mad race over the rocks, leaping from one to another, helping me when I slipped, sure-footed as a goat herself. We climbed the cliffs and explored caves, places my uncle and aunt would never have allowed me to go, and we built a huge sand castle in a little sheltered cove which she had discovered and I had never known existed.

"By the end of that afternoon, I was Marguerite's slave. She was nineteen, she told me, and I was fourteen, but the difference between us was unimportant, for either I was old for my age or she was young for hers, or it was a bit of both. She was a wonderful companion: great fun one day, serious and brooding another, but always ready to play an intriguing game according to her mood.

"Sometimes I spent whole days at the grey house. Mr Gemelli shut himself up to to write in his study and we had the place to ourselves until he joined us in the dining room for meals. He was always kind and protective towards Marguerite, and to me, too, but her attitude to him I found puzzling. She seemed to take no notice of him, as children will often ignore the grown-ups in their life, taking them for granted; but she saw to his needs and thanked him politely when he complimented her on her cooking.

"She liked cooking, she said. Food was precious, she stated solemnly as I helped her to make dainty tea-cakes in the kitchen, and she liked to treat it well. Once when she had made a cake and decorated it beautifully, she put it on a silver salver and told me to kneel down with her and worship it. I was horrified and told her it was wicked to worship anything or anyone but God. She stared at me strangely for a while, her eyes big dark pools with a far-away look in them, and then her face relaxed.

"'Of course you are right, but once food meant to me as much as God. I have no parents; they died of starvation.'

"She said no more and I didn't ask. But some time later my brother, your Uncle William, who was in the army, arrived unexpectedly when the Gemellis were visiting us. At the sight of his uniform, Marguerite gave a stifled scream, her body began to shake, and she ran to her husband. He held her very firmly in his arms, talking to her soothingly in their own language, and took her away soon afterwards.

"All that summer I visited the grey house whenever I could; sometimes my aunt and uncle came with me, but more often I went alone. Most of the time Marguerite seemed happy in the house; she liked arranging flowers and polishing the furniture and the door knocker, but everything else was attended to by a daily woman from the town. We spent a great deal of our time by the shore; Marguerite loved the seagulls and drew exquisite quick sketches of them, capturing their flight in a few graceful strokes. She told me she wished she were a seagull herself and could be free to fly out over the sea. She said that if reincarnation were true, that's what she would come back as, a seagull. Once she frightened me thoroughly by grabbing my hand as we stood on a headland, with gulls were wheeling over us in a white flutter of wings and the air full of their peculiar screeching cries. Then she threw back her head and laughed, and I shivered as I heard an echo of their cry in her laugh.

"'Come on, let's fly off this cliff and join the seagulls.'

"Later, when I told my aunt of this incident, I saw her look quickly at my uncle, and after this they almost always came with me when I visited the grey house. I loved them but regretted that their presence spoilt my comradeship with Marguerite. As summer drew to an end I knew that soon I would have to go back home to Blessington and school, and

I visited the grey house once more on my own. Marguerite stood looking out of the tall second-storey window at the sea, which was dark and stormy that day, flecked with white foam. Her husband hovered about her, anxious, and did not go to his study. When he finally left the room, Marguerite turned to me urgently, stretching out her hand.

"'Come on out... out! He won't let me out!'

"We scrambled down the stairs to the hall, but when we got to the door, he was there facing us. He put his hands on her shoulders, turning her gently back.

"One day shortly afterwards, my aunt came to me and told me sadly that Marguerite had fallen out of that second-storey window and that, although she was recovering, she might never be quite well again. She was in a private nursing home, where, it seemed, she would have to remain, and her husband had shut himself up in his study surrounded by her sketches of the sea-gulls she had loved so much.

"I was a long time getting over that sorrow, for, young as I was, I loved and understood Marguerite, and she filled an important place in my life. For a long time afterwards, I had no wish to see the grey house again. But one day during my next holidays, something made me go back. It was once more empty. Mr Gemelli had gone away.

"I walked slowly up the long avenue, which was now overgrown with weeds, the trees bent and crippled by the wind. I reached the gravel sweep and looked up at the house. It had a cold, blank stare. No frilly curtains and no flowers adorned the windows.

The paint on the front door was worn and blistered, the brass knocker was dull and greened with weathering.

"Sadly I turned to go when suddenly I saw her – Marguerite! Standing there in the second-storey window. Wearing a long white dress, she was staring away out to sea, her lovely dark hair tumbled about her shoulders. I waved and called, but she didn't seem to see me. I called again, but she didn't move.

"Then I saw the seagulls. A whole host of them came flying up from the cliffs below and circled over where I was standing, then rose up and up, towards the window, and then over the house. I saw Marguerite throw her head back and laugh, and as I heard the great answering cry from that host of seagulls, the hair rose on my head and I turned and ran.

"Bursting into the drawing room, I told my aunt breathlessly about seeing Marguerite. She turned to my uncle who was reading the evening paper.

"'The Gemellis are back... the child saw Marguerite!'

"He looked up. 'The man's mad, bringing her back there.' Suddenly he looked down and up again. 'Are you sure you saw her, child?'

"I said I was quite sure and told them again what I had seen. My uncle gazed at me curiously for a moment and then read slowly from the paper.

"'Peacefully, at Mount Collier Nursing Home, Marguerite, beloved wife of Jerome Gemelli.'"

# The Straight Furrow

ONE DAY WHEN Philippa and Helen were playing tennis at the local tennis club, Mother asked me to take Robert – home for the summer holidays – and Jenny for a walk out of the way of painters coming to work in the house. I didn't mind, relishing the responsibility and the freedom to take them wherever I wished. There were so many lovely places around Ardglass, always within reach or view of the sea. I decided we'd go to the golf links which ran around the cliffs to a place called Ringfad Point, and we set out on a lane which ran alongside the links.

Spotting a seagull standing on the stone dyke, we crept up as close as we could without disturbing it. Then Robert made a jump at it, laughing, and it flew away. We watched it swooping across the golf links towards the sea, and soon it was lost in the shining whiteness of that summer day. We continued on along the dyke, grey stones laid upon grey stones, all shapes and sizes seemingly set haphazardly upon each other, yet secure, with ferns and grasses and tufts of campion growing between. We wandered along, plucking the grasses and chewing them, until Robert called us to a place where he'd climbed a stone wall. On the other side lay a small wood, within which we could make out a dilapidated stone farm house around which a crowd of flustered fowl were squawking near the door. As we watched, a shower of meal was thrown out and quietened them as they pecked the mud path clean. Below the house in a clearing amongst the trees, a pond lurked invitingly.

"A muck pond," Robert announced, clearly interested. A figure emerged from the house and threw something from a bucket into the murky water. The figure then turned and regarded us. An old woman, I thought, not sure at first because of the man's cap on her head; then, not so old, I concluded as several children joined her. She wore big Wellington boots, a sack tied round her waist and her hair tucked into her cap.

A little farther on a boy was leaning on the gate to the farm, sucking a straw. His eyes were all I was aware of, very dark and intense, with thick dark brows above them. He smiled shyly as we passed. Later I mentioned the incident to father.

"It's a queer, sad sort of place and there's a lot of children; they must be Catholics," I said.

"They're not, they're Protestants; ours in fact, Church of Ireland," my father informed me, taking off his hat and coat after conducting his visits around the parish. "And Mrs Creighton tells me you're very cheeky children. She says you were all sitting on the wall of her farm, staring and making remarks. 'Very cheeky children you have, your Reverence,' she said to me. Now isn't that a nice way, disgracing me in my parish!"

I was indignant.

"Queer old thing," I answered, "with a man's cap on her head!"

"Aye, they're an untidy lot at that farm," Father agreed, "but the eldest girl has promise. I want to try to persuade them to let her go on with her education."

"Have they a father?" I asked.

"Oh yes, but he's an alcoholic, I gather. The only yield the farm ever gives is due to the work the boy does. He's had to do the father's work and missed out on his education. They've only the one boy and five girls. I haven't seen the boy. He was away after stray sheep when I was there."

"I saw him," I said.

Mother called Father then and I slipped out.

The Creighton boy was at the gate again. When I reached it, he climbed over to my side. We began to walk towards the sea. A fishing boat was coming in and the gulls were screeching over it, a greedy rush of sharp beaks and white wings. Farther out more boats were following, coming home with herring for the market and for tea. We exchanged our names that day, that was all. His name was Davie.

From that day on I always met Davie at his gate. His mother stopped calling us cheeky children. Indeed, she was so grateful to Father for taking an interest in her Elizabeth that she put on a proper hat and came to church. But I never let her see me with Davie. Usually we went to where the sheep were pastured, away at the end of the golf links in a rough hillocky place. We'd sit at the edge of the sea, sometimes with our bare feet in it, and watch the water redden as the sun went down, or the summer moon making dark eerie shapes out of the furze bushes. Davie told me frightening stories to tease me, or made up poetry, which he recited to me.

"Little white face like the campion flower,
hair that's bloom of gorse."

"But I haven't yellow hair," I protested.

Some of his poetry was incomprehensible but some of it was good, and I felt a special sense of sharing of experience between us as I listened to him.

I didn't ask Davie how old he was; perhaps he was about seventeen. He was tall, but he looked young, except sometimes when he was tired; his eyes would be sad then, and have an old look in them. Sometimes he was in a bad mood, surly and quiet, and he would cry about nothing, like a baby. He never cried when his father cuffed him, though I wished he would cry then so that I could comfort him. But after a row in the house, he'd be dreamy and sweet and the poetry he recited would become gentler and more incomprehensible than usual.

Not allowed to stay out late, I ran home, grabbed my tennis racquet where I'd left it at the farm gate, and concocted lies to tell about the games I had won. But I experienced no guilty conscience. Davie was right in my world, even if he was only a farm labourer.

When spring came Davie had more to do on the farm. Soon he was engrossed in lambing and calving and sowing and ploughing and I helped him after school. One of the things he liked me to do was to stand on the stone dyke as he ploughed towards me so that he got the furrow straight. There was no machinery on that farm, and Davie followed the plough with a cumbersome but obedient old horse in the shafts. Keeping me in sight between the horse's ears, Davie would plough the furrow as straight as a die. I soon tired of having to run up the muddy field to be in his sights for his return journey, and so I only consented to stay put on the dyke, just moving along a pace when I saw him turn to come back. As a result crooked and straight furrows alternated across the field.

One evening that spring, Davie wasn't at the gate. Then he called to me from beyond the house. He said there was nobody at home and he had to stay handy because a cow was ready to calve. I had never been so close to the house before. Now I could see that the curtains were dirty and bags of meal lay on the kitchen floor. A hen wandered in through the open door. Outside, one of the children's broken go-carts was sticking out of the pond.

Davie took my hand and hauled me up into a tree that had a good seat, a big wide bowl in the centre where the branches divided. As it was early spring, the leaves were just unfolding, clean green and a little creased. I turned my back on the muck pond.

Suddenly there was an uproar. The farm dog and another scallywag of a dog that belonged to the tinkers were fighting each other right in the middle of all the hens. Feathers flew and the barking and squawking must have been heard a mile away. Davie just laughed. Then suddenly he jumped down, threw his own dog in the pond and chased the tinkers' dog over the wall.

After recovering from kinks of laughter that gave me pains, we were lying quiet, stretched out along the smooth round branches. I turned my head sideways, my cheek against the satin-smooth skin of the tree, and saw close to my face a bursting bud. The unfurled spear of leaves thrust up, pale whitish green with a pinkish tinge at the tip, from the grip of the stalk that held it. Something stirred in me – discontent, discomfort, even pain – and I was crying. I looked for Davie to comfort me.

Suddenly I heard him laugh. He was sitting astride his branch throwing bits of bark at the dogs. He looked at me.

"I must go home," I announced sitting up.

"It's the sap rising," he said, an unfamiliar smile on his face. "That's why you're crying."

Suddenly he reached for me, and I jumped. I landed among the dogs and they separated and ran, yelping.

"What you go spoiling their fun for?" Davie called after me, laughing again as I climbed the gate. He followed me slowly and stood facing me across it. He was different, not soft or vulnerable, not even young any more.

Father was waiting for me when I reached home.

"You've been seeing that Creighton boy," he accused.

For what seemed like hours, my father ranted on. Mother cried, declaring that I'd grow up badly and it was all her fault because she was so poorly and couldn't look after me. It appeared that one of the children had found out and split on me. There was no use explaining. My parents' fears and apprehension coincided with my own bewilderment at the sudden change in Davie.

So it was arranged for me to go to boarding school, and one evening I went to the farm to tell Davie that I was to start the next term at a school in Dublin. I might as well have said Timbuktu, so far was Dublin from that little northern town to a boy like Davie. Gone was all the new-found manhood, and he was once again the boy I'd known, ready to cry like the great baby I'd so often called him.

"I *have* to go," I said as I left him, only a little reluctantly.

The day I set off with my father on the first leg of my journey to Dublin, I sat in the little train that had carried me to day school, and chose the side where I could see the trees of the Creighton farm on the sky line. And there against the clouds I saw him, standing behind the old-fashioned plough. A host of seagulls dived and soared above the upturned earth. He waved towards the train. My father took no notice: country people always waved at trains. But suddenly I remembered the hillocky place and realised that I wouldn't be sitting there with my feet in the sea, and I thought tearfully, "Oh Davie, Davie, will you ever plough a straight furrow without me?"

*The straight furrow*

# First Day at Boarding School

I CONSOLED MYSELF with the thought that going to a prestigious school in Dublin made me important. The prospect even seemed exciting. I looked forward to midnight feasts and meeting other girls coming from all over Ireland. I had packed my trunk with all my treasured possessions: favourite books, a new hockey stick and lacrosse and tennis racquets. I looked at these sporting items with trepidation. Unlike my sister Helen, I was no good at games,.

When Father and I reached Dublin, we sent my trunk on to the school and spent several hours in second-hand bookshops – dusty, dark, fascinating places in his old haunts around Trinity College and down the quays. But the fascination could not hold my interest, for I was eager to explore my new destiny.

"When are we going to my school?" I asked, wearily trotting after him.

"We'll go this very afternoon," he promised absently, placing a pile of books with satisfaction on the counter and commencing to bargain with the proprietor over the price. Eventually, a deal having been negotiated, we left the shop and went to a butcher's in Henry Street.

"There's nothing to beat Haffner's sausages," said Father happily.

Back we went to Nassau Street and the Kylemore Bakery, for a fruit loaf which Mother loved, and from there we walked up Grafton Street to Bewley's where the aroma of roasting coffee beans wafted a welcome as exotic as the designation above the door of "Oriental Restaurant". Inside I happily tucked into delicious sticky buns washed down with piping hot coffee.

From Grafton Street it was a short walk through St Stephen's Green to Earlsfort Terrace, where Alexandra School and College stood, imposing elegant red-brick buildings along one side of the street. At the end of the terrace stood a tall grey building; this was Number 12, the Clergy Daughters' School, except that it wasn't a school; it was a residence for Alexandra School and College, and the staff of the Clergy Daughters' School were housemistresses rather than teachers. Opposite stood the National University, made of more grey stone. My heart slipped a little downwards. As we mounted the steps up to the front door of the building at the end of the terrace, I noticed a high wall surrounding a bit of grass at the side.

When a uniformed maid opened the door, I could see my trunk sitting forlornly in the hall, my name on the label. Suddenly I shivered. The maid knocked on a door on the right and smiled at me in a timorous way until a lady came out. She was short and square, as austere as the polished hall in which we were standing. Looking at her fob watch, an ornate thing on a chain, she announced firmly, "You are late."

Father, prepared to be his usual affable self, was taken aback. He fumbled inside his coat and brought out his big gold watch on its chain. He consulted it.

"Two minutes late," he agreed. "I apologise. We were sampling the delights of my native city. Is it yours, mam?" He inquired politely.

The austerity melted a little.

"It is indeed a beautiful city."

She turned to me, as a big girl in a very short brown gym dress and brown stockings came through a door at the back of the hall.

"Ellen will show you your dormitory, while I talk to your father."

I looked back at Father, but met the stern gaze of the lady. I meekly followed Ellen, who took me through lino-covered dun-coloured corridors and up several flights of stairs to a big long room with the name "Mountain View" on the door. I rushed to one of the tall windows. All I could see were roofs and tall chimneys.

"Where is the mountain?" I cried.

Ellen looked at me sympathetically. "I come from the country, too, far in the north, near Londonderry."

She came beside me and pointed. "See away between those two buildings: it's misty today, but there's a mountain there."

"What's your dormitory called?" I asked.

"Star Chamber, up the next flight. You can see the stars on a starry night. Here's your trunk. I'll help you unpack."

Two maids had hauled it up the stairs. I smiled at them, went to say "thank you", but noticed that

Ellen took no notice of them. They left abruptly.

"We're not allowed to talk to any of the servants," Ellen explained.

"Goodness!" I was astonished. "Ours were always our friends."

Ellen shrugged. "This is a very Victorian establishment," she pronounced loftily, "everybody in their place."

"Do you like it?" I asked doubtfully.

"Oh it's okay, a place to eat and sleep. But school's great, so's college. My sister's there, has a good time, and she's going to Trinity next year. Come on, this is your bed. Put your things in this locker."

I surveyed my sleeping quarters, with the brown linoleum-covered floor, six black iron bedsteads, mine beside the door, brown paint half way up the walls, then faded green to the high ceiling. There was one electric light with a green shade. The effect was dismal.

Suddenly I bolted for the door, raced along the corridor, down the front stairs, through a door into the front hall where my father was still standing with the principal.

"Daddy, Daddy!" I cried throwing my arms around his neck.

He hugged me and whispered. "Be a good girl. I'll come down soon again to see you."

The principal, taken momentarily aback at my flying interruption, asserted her authority. "Come now, no nonsense," she said, placing a heavy hand on my shoulder. She indicated Ellen, who had come anxiously after me: "Go with Ellen, in to tea now.

Goodbye, Mr Draper." Almost pushing my father out, she firmly shut the heavy door after him.

Tea consisted of white bread, cut thick, three pats of butter and some very watery greengage jam. I found I couldn't eat.

"Do you not want your tea?" the girl beside me asked.

I shook my head and she gleefully took my slice and gobbled it hungrily.

"We'll not get anything more until supper," she said. "My name is Daffodil, Daffodil Clements."

She talked with her mouth full and I wondered if I had heard her right. Daffodil! Daisy, Iris, Primrose, Lily, yes, but Daffodil! And Daffodil it was.

"Next time there's something you like on my plate you can have it. Sometimes there's strawberry jam, yum, yum, yum."

I began to feel better, especially as it turned out that she was sleeping next to me in the dormitory.

"I've got some sweets under my pillow," she whispered.

After tea we were free to do as we pleased until supper. There was a library of sorts, along half a wall in the "prep" room where we did our homework. I had brought my own favourite reading matter, including a set of the "Anne" books by L. M. Montgomery and the "Emily" trilogy. The comfort of these trusty friends in the sudden bleakness that came over me was immeasurable.

I couldn't eat at supper time either that first night. The soup had a burnt taste, and the white bread was accompanied by no butter this time.

Daffodil helped me with mine.

"It's mostly always singed," she said, dipping the bread into my plate of greyish liquid. "I think the cook they employ here is in training."

A dish of bananas and custard with watery red jam on top appeared. The principal dished it out and then went back to her table where the staff of four house-mistresses were eating something that smelled much more savoury than our meal. I ate the bananas out of my helping and Daffodil ate the rest.

"Did you bring anything for a feast?" the girl opposite whispered.

"A cake, but I've eaten a bit of it already," Daffodil giggled, her mouth full.

They looked at me.

"I didn't know you had feasts at the beginning of term," I apologised, "but I've got some apples."

"That'll do. Everybody brings something. Phyllis has a whole cooked chicken and I've got a chocolate cake."

As we rose from the table, Phyllis leaned across to me. "We feast at midnight," she whispered.

I brightened. It had begun to feel more like the boarding schools I'd read about. At midnight the dormitory quietly came alive. We had a monitress, an older girl who had a screen round her bed a little apart from ours. I envied her her privacy and thought of my little room at home in Ardglass with its view of the Delectable Mountains and I began to cry. Daffodil cut a big slice of chocolate cake and gave it to me.

"Here now, eat that and don't spoil the fun."

She slapped me on the back, and I dried my eyes

on my pyjamas and took a bite of cake.

We sat on the floor in the middle of the dorm with all the goodies spread on a towel. Our monitress was a decent sort and went to see a friend who was a monitress in another dormitory.

I had a chicken leg in one hand and the chocolate cake in the other when a fat girl called Lizzy, who was, it seemed, a junior house-mistress, stormed in.

"This is not allowed!" she declared triumphantly, grabbing the four corners of the towel and sweeping our eats all up together. We demurred but she was adamant.

"I could overlook it if it was the end of term, when you could be sick in the train or the car going home, but not here, and with school tomorrow."

She swept out. We looked sadly at what we had in our hands.

"But she eats it all herself. She's as fat as Tweedle Dum."

"She hasn't got it all," Daffodil announced softly. She had been sitting on a cake tin, her dressing gown draped over it. Inside was most of a Victoria sandwich. She divided it up amongst us just as our monitress came back. We jumped into bed munching solidly, alternately cake and chicken leg.

"I might be sick," I whispered, offering my cake to Daffodil.

"Don't you dare!" she hissed. "What a waste that'd be when I could have had it."

"It's a wonder you're not as fat as Tweedle Dum yourself," her neighbour in the next bed taunted. "You're never full."

"Hollow legs, me dad calls me," Daffodil replied smugly, "when he isn't calling me Beanpole."

"No talking now," the monitress called. "Goodnight all."

We chorused goodnight and, after some last munching and rustling, silence descended.

There were no curtains at the tall windows and I strained my eyes searching for the mountain. I could make out only chimneys and a dark sky devoid of stars.

# Coming to Terms With It

IENDURED MY first term alternately in homesick tears and making friends with Daffodil and Pat, Una and Daphne, girls who had come to the school a year earlier than I had. As they had experienced homesickness themselves, they were sympathetic in their way, but told me to snap out of it. On Sundays I wrote letters home, supervised, with the rest of the boarders, by a member of staff or a senior girl. At first I wrote long tear-smudged epistles to my father telling him how I hated the place and what gorgons the house-mistresses were. I complained about the awful food and the crocodile walks around the lake in St Stephen's Green and along Baggot Street canal, threatening that I would jump in to end the misery of it all.

Certain that my letters would be steamed open by school censors, I tore them up. A religious mistress, observing that I spent so much of my first term weeping, patted me on the head and assured me it was God's will. She didn't enquire as to the reason for my tears or offer any help, and her observation only made me hate the God I had loved as a child. Church services presented another problem, for they were always long and boring. We endured the experience in seats at the front of the church, flanked by prefects at the end of each pew, while the principal

91

sat at the back of our block in a commanding position from which she could spot the smallest deviation from the rigid behaviour expected of us.We were not allowed to whisper or eat sweets; an exception was made for cough sweets, but these were rationed, and were anyway so horrible that they didn't constitute a temptation. The inevitably lengthy sermon always passed high above our heads.

At home in Ardglass Philippa played golf with a nice deaf lady in the parish.and was good at the sign language for the deaf. I had picked up an amount myself so that I could converse with her too. Now in school, knowing the signs for the alphabet, I began to show them to the girl beside me, furtively. Soon we were engrossed, hands working below the pew, heads together. A nudge came along the pew from the prefect at the end, but it came too late, for the principal had seen and I was sent for after lunch. She was fuming.

"You would hardly behave like that in the presence of His Majesty the King! How much more reprehensible in the presence of the King of Kings!"

I couldn't see the relevance of this, as we were surely in the Free State, not in the United Kingdom. I opened my mouth to argue, but stopped abruptly as she stood up, her eyes flashing. I hung my head and looked suitably chastened. For punishment I was not allowed into afternoon tea, which on Sundays comprised the luxury of currant cake and lemonade. I went instead up to my dormitory where I settled down to sulk on my bed. Then the door opened and there was Daffodil, with a slice of cake and lemonade in a toothmug. I could always depend on Daffodil.

During my second term at school, I got measles and was confined to my bed in the sick bay, which was right at the top of the building, looking out over Harcourt Street. I had a high temperature and was restless and miserable. My father came to visit me and I begged him to take me home to Mother, but the doctor advised against so long a journey.

People were kind, even the principal, who donned a white coat like the doctor and brought me books and fruit. It rained incessantly and I looked out on roofs of grey blue slates shining in the rain. A barrel organ played far down in the street below, plaintive sad melodies that drifted up to me – "Home Sweet Home", "The Last Rose of Summer" and "Danny Boy". I asked one of the maids who brought me my food to give the barrel organ player my sixpence pocket money for that week to play something cheerful for me. From then on he played "Dancing in the Rain" every day, and soon I was fully recovered and able to leave the sick bay.

Returning home at the end of that term, my trunk safely stowed in the guard's van, I shortened the journey by talking with several other northern girls. All of us were cheerful and glad to be going home for the holidays.

Arriving home, Mother greeted me with concern in her expression. I was pale and thin after the measles, but it was such a relief to talk to her and tell her all my unhappiness that I soon began to feel well again.

"But if you are so unhappy you cannot learn," she said anxiously. "Would you really rather go back to Down High with the others?"

I considered carefully, remembered Daffodil and the rest of the friends I had made; the art class where I was good; the dramatic society in which I excelled; well-taught English literature classes and acting out Shakespeare's plays. I thought of the trips to the Abbey and Gate theatres for half-term treats with other girls who also lived too far away to go home for the short breaks. I elected to go back. Mother was glad. She liked my new accent. And Father breathed a sigh of relief. But I did ask Mother if I could board somewhere else instead of No 12, maybe in Alexandra Residence where the girls had lovely little two-bed rooms, which were much prettier and cosier than our stark dormitories in Clergy Daughters' School. Sadly she said that Father couldn't afford it. Clergy Daughters' School was subsidised, another of the bargains he was renowned for. I never mentioned the subject again.

Back at the school, life was made possible by friendship, but it was a bit like a ship on a long voyage. Friendships were intense, and there was no privacy; enemies became almost dangerous in the enclosed atmosphere, and at an age when our attention would have been more healthily directed towards boys, it turned on ourselves. Girls loved girls, sometimes mistresses. Silly little intimacies developed. I found this sickening, especially when I discovered I had a follower in the shape of small fat new girl. Like a "fag" in a boy's public school, she wanted to do everything for me: to carry my books, fetch things for me, make my bed, brush my hair. I was cruel in my rejection of her attentions, but she soon found another girl to fawn on, who was happy to take advantage of her eagerness. As for the rest of my contemporaries, at the end of our school days, we went our ways to far-away places and, except for a few, never saw each other again. A few, still school-girls at heart, joined Old Girls Associations, living the rivalries and tensions over again, pretending their schooldays had been the best years of their lives. Even fifty years later, they still greeted each other: "My dear, you haven't changed a bit!"

On one occasion the baser of us entertained the hope that Number 12 would go up in a merry blaze. A girl warming her vest on the only means of heat in her dormitory, an oil stove, set the place on fire, and as we heard the fire bell we scrambled to our stations. But momentary pleasure vanished when I remembered my precious books and little treasures, and I wept. A house mistress thought I was overcome by love of the place. It was only a small fire, but the girl whose offending vest had started it was so thoroughly reprimanded and disgraced in front of the assembled company that she left of her own accord and went to another school somewhere in the west of Ireland. (In later life I learned that she eventually became a headmistress herself, and, contrary to expectations, ran a cosy establishment with waiting lists.)

Day school and college were reached first through

a playground between No 12 and the school, then through the college gardens which were very lovely and often proved a place of solace for me. But it meant we never had to go out into Earlsfort Terrace. Not much chance of escape, I thought glumly more than once when I contemplated the dun brown corridors and linoleum of No 12, pervaded with the smell of turnip and cabbage boiled too long.

We played hockey against Catholic schools, often convents down in the Wicklow countryside, and the teas we got in the convents afterwards were lovely, consisting of mouth-watering fancy sandwiches, sausage rolls and cakes. The nuns were nice to us and the girls seemed to be quite happy in their environment.

"I wish I was a Catholic," I announced on my return from one such hockey outing as I contemplated another appearance of our interminable banana custard. "They get much better food than we do."

One day we were all summoned to the great hall for the expulsion of two girls. The entire staff sat on the platform in their black gowns and academic hoods. The two girls were summoned to stand in front of the assembled staff and the headmistress spoke quietly to them; then she pointed to the door. They had to walk the length of the great hall in complete silence and continue out of the door to where their grieving and shocked parents waited to take them away. Tears poured down the faces of their classmates and one teacher fainted. Afterwards we went to our classrooms almost afraid to speak. What *had* they done, was the question in all our minds.

"Must have murdered somebody!" I suggested and was immediately suppressed. It was never spoken of again, but I often wondered what happened to those two girls.

I was keen on the Girl Guides, especially because of camping trips to Powerscourt some weekends, which offered a wonderful escape from the usual routine; and the food – sausage stew cooked over an open fire – tasted unforgettably good to my palate. Unfortunately, however, I didn't get on with the Guide captain, a Miss Wallace, who was also a housemistress. She took a dim view of me, insisting after I had been in trouble a couple of times that I "let my imagination run away with me, resulting in downright lies".

It was indeed my imagination that had got me into trouble, but I didn't like to be called a liar. When I had first arrived in the school, I had dreamed that I could dance, floating like a fairy in *Giselle* or partnering Fred Astaire in a glorious routine of rapid ballroom steps. In reality we were taught Irish dancing once a week in the dining room by a beautiful tall girl in a green tunic. At my first class she got each of us up in turn to show her what we could do. Some of the southern girls had learned Irish dancing at home, but we from the north had not had the opportunity. Nevertheless, I was convinced that I could dance – "The Waves of Tory" looked easy. When she asked me to demonstrate, I made such a fool of myself that I cried for hours afterwards.

The teacher was kind, saying, "Never mind, I'll

teach you." But Miss Wallace, when she heard of it, declared that I was a liar.

On another occasion we were given a summer holiday competition to research any foreign country of our choice which we thought we might like to visit. Some of the girls were going abroad and one or two even lived abroad, so they could carry out their researches there. For my part I chose Egypt and I researched it so thoroughly, cutting out pieces from travel magazines and visiting the library to read about the history of the pyramids, the clothes and the music of Egypt, both ancient and modern, that I imagined that I really had visited the country. So effective was my presentation that I won the competition, but later when it emerged that I had not in fact visited my wonderful, exotic destination, I was again denounced as a liar and thoroughly humiliated.

Now I had to face a sort of confessional test which formed part of one's continued membership of the Guides. I resented this intrusion upon a privacy which was very hard to maintain in the best of circumstances as a boarder, and, to make matters worse, my tester was the Guide captain, Miss Wallace. The inquisition took place in her bedroom at 6.30 in the morning, where she sat, warm and cosy, in her bed while I, the unfortunate Guide, half-washed and half-awake, had to sit on the end of her bed and answer her questions. The atmosphere was too intimate for me. I shivered with dislike, and I knew she didn't like me.

"Do you tell lies?" she asked me sternly.

My continued membership of the Guides hung on my answer. But I was older now, perhaps a little harder. I held up my head. This stern woman in a Victorian nightdress, high-necked and long-sleeved, all tucks and lace insertions in the bodice accentuating her flat chest, was not going to intimidate me.

She asked again, scarcely stifling a yawn, "Do you tell lies?"

"No, not deliberately," I replied.

"What does that mean?" she challenged me.

"My imagination takes me by surprise sometimes," I endeavoured to explain, adding in my mind: "Thank goodness for it, in this place!"

"Well, you must keep it under control," she admonished, glaring at me. Then, yawning again, she dismissed me.

I knew she was right, but as I looked back from the door, I thought wryly, "I'll bet you would never dream of dancing with Fred Astaire."

akes which tethered his two

loose!" she exclaimed on her

, Father hurried after them,
several fields away and reluc-
r newly acquired freedom. As
utside, the evening continued
11 o'clock, Mother's deadline,
ed none too subtly by playing
to signal that it was time for
ome. As Father had rounded
me, he was not grudged a few
ests were leaving.

riends was now tolerated, but
d to have Catholic boyfriends.
1 a very good-looking young
village, I asked belligerently,
stians, same as we are!"

lt enough estate to enter into
e so by marrying out of your
u, they wouldn't like it any
ther replied.

newly arrived in Ardglass,
ing along with us, the four
we had stopped to talk to a
he knew. As their conversa-
se, the man had looked at us
e growing up in Ardglass, will

lded, he had answered firmly,
ns!"

# Holidays

A S TERM NEARED its end, the prospect of going
home for the holidays ushered in a wonderful
and exciting period of anticipation. However, I
was finding that going home only three times a year
was isolating me in part from my family, and also
from my community. Robert found this, too, and he
complained that his sisters were becoming strangers
to him. We for our part decided he was too much of a
stranger to impose silly tricks upon and so we
stopped the teasing with which we used to plague
him. Since his school friends had scattered to their
homes across the province, he found the holidays
lonely and trying. Except for sitting on Mother's bed
and telling her all about his separate life at school,
he had nothing to do except wander down to the harbour and watch the fishing boats and their crews.
He always cheered up when the end of the holidays
came and Father drove him up to Belfast and school
again.

I, too, found that I was often lonely in the holidays. Philippa and Helen had friends at school in
Downpatrick and the surrounding countryside and
were often invited out. Helen played hockey for the
school and latterly for Ulster, so was fully occupied
with important matches. Philippa devoted most of
her time to golf and to playing the organ in church.

She had been unhappy at school and Father had let her leave; after all, he needed her at home to help him look after Mother. Mary hadn't been replaced when she married her boyfriend, and the rectory had become a sad and neglected house. Jenny, returning home from school, would find nobody in except Mother, chained to her bed, impotent and unhappy. Jenny would make her a cup of tea and herself a slice of bread and jam, and then Philippa, coming in from golf, would get the evening meal ready. She was kind and gentle with Mother, and the evenings when we were all in the house seemed brighter.

But I noticed differences every time I came home. Father wasn't well himself; he was often "taking turns", Mother said, and eating far too much: "comfort eating" she called it. "He has so much to worry about: me in this helpless state, the two parishes to look after. The doctor says his heart isn't too good, but he won't listen to the doctor."

I found that he had become more irascible and dogmatic than before.

"If I say the moon is made of green cheese, it is made of green cheese!" He shouted at us.

The unfortunate result of his bad temper was that none of us took anything he said seriously. Rows and arguments ensued. We were growing up and he couldn't accept it. He had become paranoid about boyfriends, Philippa and Helen said. They knew several boys about the place and were both very pretty. I could only envy them. I had no boyfriend. Where would I meet one, after all, incarcerated as I was in a female institution.

and pulled up the goats.

"Dad, the goats a return.

Fussing and fumi but by now they wer tant to surrender th Father chased them inside as planned un which Philippa conve the National Anthem the boys to be going up the goats by that minutes' chat as the

The existence of bo we were not encourag

As I had my eye Catholic fellow in the "Why not? They're Ch

"Marriage is a diffic without making it m own kind. I assure more than I would," F

Once when we ha Father had been dri girls, in the car when Catholic teacher who tion had drawn to a c and asked, "Will they ye tell me?"

When Father had n "I'm off to lock up my

# The Final Year

A T THE END of one holiday, I became anxious about the situation at home. Both parents were ill now, and Philippa couldn't cope with everything. Mother worried about her.

"She's too quiet, and lonely."

Plenty of boys admired her, especially the summer visitors, for she had grown very beautiful. But she had become shy and her only recreation now was to play golf with the deaf lady.

I wondered if I should leave Dublin and come home to help look after things. I asked Mother, regressing in my anxiety to the childish mode of addressing my parents.

"Oh, Mammy, with you and Daddy ill, should I not come home?"

"Finish your education, Alana," she answered, using the pet name she had for us all, from the Irish "leanbh" for "child." "You've been doing well and it's too precious to lose."

I was glad it was decided for me. I had only another year to go.

When I passed from school into college and was able to wear "mufti" instead of my shabby, shiny, brown gym dress and brown lyle stockings, I became a new girl, confident and assured. College only required us to wear the blazer, a splendid red with a white and silver crest on the pocket. We felt like university students, and most of us aspired to go on to Trinity or the National in Dublin, Queen's in Belfast or Foyle in Londonderry. The westerners went to Galway, Limerick or Cork, while some, of wealthier parents, went to England.

I became a prefect and life improved enormously. Not only did I now have privacy of a sort, with curtains around my bed, but I was also allowed out! On Saturday mornings I headed happily for Grafton Street with a list of 'tuck' to buy for the younger children spending their weekly sixpences. I explored as much of Dublin as I could in the time: Wicklow Street, Dawson Street, Nassau Street; in Grafton Street I had a coffee in Bewleys and looked at the lovely clothes in Switzers and Brown Thomas. Clutching a little money gathered from birthday and Christmas gifts, I could run away now, I thought, get on the train on a one-way ticket and go home. And then I knew I didn't want to. This was my city, as it had been my father's. I loved it. I browsed in a couple of 'his' second-hand bookshops, before venturing to Woolworths to buy the 'tuck' of Fry's chocolate bars, humbugs, liquorice all-sorts and Rowntree's fruit gums. Sixpence went a long way. Next port of call was the Kylemore Bakery at the end of Nassau Street where I bought a sweet sticky cake to share with my friends. I walked back to No 12 Earlsfort Terrace, reconciled, for the time being anyway, to my life as a scholar.

I began to recognise that the education provided by both school and college was splendid, even if the discipline was strict. The curriculum was broad and comprehensive, with a definite English influence. Armistice Day was observed, an important occasion in the calendar, and we attended the solemn and sad remembrance, where I noticed a teacher dressed in black who wore, just on that day, a beautiful ring on her engagement finger.

We had to learn Irish: a government subsidy was involved and we could not achieve certificates of education unless we passed exams in it. The young Irish teacher was nervous and made the language class dull; four of us northerners sat in the back row of the classroom paying scant attention and did the minimum of study, but in the face of our uninterested front the teacher just raised her eyebrows and shrugged her shoulders. We learned enough to pass our exams, but I felt later in life that we lost out more than we imagined at the time, for Irish is a language rich in rhythm and colour and best learned when young.

We read English history thoroughly, and a smattering of Irish history, which was enough to whet my appetite for more. I was both indignant and astonished when our headmistress told us not to forget that we had enjoyed the privilege of being educated at 'the Girton of Ireland'. I would have preferred to think of it as 'the flower of Ireland', or even 'the crown of Ireland', though such a description might be challenged by other establishments. I told my father about it, but he only laughed. All the same, I found that I now enjoyed the happy atmosphere of Alexandra, which encouraged in me good behaviour and a desire to learn.

I also delighted, in my trips into the city, finding in the second hand bookshops books such as *The Great Hunger* by Cecil Woodham-Smith and *Constance Markievicz* by Sean O'Faolain which gave me a new and fascinating perspective. I admired Constance for her courage and concern for the poor of Ireland, though I didn't care for Maud Gonne, another patriot, for making a monkey out of W. B. Yeats the way she had, and he such a wonderful poet. She hadn't, I felt, deserved his adulation, expressed in unforgettable poetry inspired by his love for her and for his country.

"Rose of all Roses, Rose of all the World!
You too, have come where the dim tides
are hurled
Upon the waves of sorrow, and heard ring
The bell that calls us on; the sweet far thing.
Beauty grown sad with its eternity
Made you of us, and of the dim grey sea."

These lines haunted me as a teenager: I thought I heard the ringing of the bell that calls us on, the sweet far thing, the searching, the longing. How awful, I thought, if that bell ever stopped ringing.

Once I saw Maud Gonne walking down Grafton Street. She was tall, old and gaunt, dressed in black with a chiffon widow's veil trailing after her. Everybody looked, for she was still beautiful.

When I went home for the holiday after that term, Mother said my choice of reading was far too heavy for me. She gave me *Never No More* by Maura Laverty, a beautiful and gently educational book for a growing girl, but I still liked to delve into the lives

108

of idealists and heroes and heroines of old, and the poetry they inspired.

In our final term a dance was held for all those due to leave, a posh affair in the beautiful Jellicoe Hall of the college, so named in honour of a Quaker girl who had worked for women's education in the 1800s and became the founder and first lady superintendent of Alexandra School and College.

Brothers sufficed for our partners on the night, or students of Trinity, the school having a preference for divinity students, which caused my father to chuckle at his memories of his own time in the divinity school. I knew only one such student at the time, the son of a neighbouring clergyman from home. I didn't care for him much. Small and stout, he struck me as unprepossessing and I disliked the fact that his initials were WC. But I wanted to go to the ball and so, reluctantly, I wrote and asked him. He wrote accepting my invitation "with pleasure" and I set about making myself a ball gown.

I wrote now to Father requesting, if he could afford it, two pounds to buy the material for a dress. He obliged and Mother sent me a pink satin petticoat of her own. I went as soon as I could to Brown Thomas in Grafton Street and bought several yards of pink net. Then I sewed an off-the-shoulder full-skirted dress, all by hand. It fitted perfectly, the satin shine through the net and the skirt had a perfect swirl. I pictured myself waltzing the night away, and if I shut my eyes, I thought, WC might turn into a handsome prince. I nursed a spot on my chin all week, and when it disappeared on the day of the dance, I took it as a good omen. We were all so excited that it was as well that our exams were over, for we could concentrate on nothing else.

The hall was decorated with imported palms, flowers in abundance and arrangements of coloured leaves and berries in the windows and on marble mantelpieces throughout the college, the work of one of the teachers. A band played real dance music, but alas, my partner could not dance. So we sat out under the palms between sorties to the supper tables, which were set with delicious canapés and sandwiches, assorted bridge rolls, which I had helped to fill earlier in the day, and all sorts of cakes. Only non-alcoholic drinks were available to us, but I caught sight of members of staff carrying sherry and port into a room in which they stayed playing bridge all evening.

At one stage I forced my partner on to the floor, determined to teach him to waltz. A lovely, graceful girl and her partner went whirling by with great panache.

"See, like that!" I hissed.

He did his best to please me, but he trod on my toes repeatedly; soon we retired to the sidelines again to watch the dancers. The lovely girl and her handsome partner came drifting by, taking the floor, while others danced around the edge of the hall. The girl wore a gown of green shot silk with a halter neck, her smooth creamy back bare. I knew her as Sarah and I admired her enormously, from her blonde hair to her height and grace; she was everything I wanted to be. As her partner held her tightly

110

and deftly turned her round and round, their heads thrown back as they laughed into each other's faces, suddenly her dress slipped sideways, exposing one breast, beautiful with its dark aureole.

There was an audible gasp and someone hissed, "Adjust your dress!"

Sarah looked down, then hurriedly pulling her dress straight, her golden hair falling over her flushed face, she ran from the room. Her partner, equally flushed and perturbed, followed her.

The dancing continued, but the festivities had become subdued and never recovered their lively spirit.

Sarah was in the cloakroom when I went to get my coat. She was crying, her eyes, so recently flashing with laughter and happiness, were red and swollen.

"It wasn't such a terrible thing," I said to her. "I wish I could dance as well as you do."

The dance over, WC walked me up to Number 12 and we stood on the steps saying goodnight. He was a perfect gentleman, thanking me for the invitation, saying how much he had enjoyed the evening. I felt fully seventeen going on eighteen. He rang the door-bell for me.

The principal opened the heavy door. "Come in at once, you little goose," she commanded waspishly. And my sense of well-being came crashing down around me.

In bed I couldn't sleep. I tried to read, then got out a notebook and put my hurt feelings down on paper, writing to two literary girls with whom I felt a special empathy.

Dear Charlotte and Emily,

How I sympathise with you, sent to that awful school! I am at one like Lowood, for clergy daughters, where discipline is all the rule. Subsidised, bare and loveless in stern Victorian style. Love and understanding are not thought to be a requisite for learning, nor kindness necessary.

And oh, the cold is dire! Once a shivering girl warming her vest on an oil stove set the dormitory on fire. Did you get enough to eat? Emily, you were small like me: what did you get for tea? White bread and watered jam for my hunger, two pats of butter, and burnt soup for supper. Were there maids at your school? We aren't allowed to fraternise. But I am "left of middle" even still and call to the basement where they live – "Hello, hello, you should rebel" – sorry for their lowly, darkened lives. These are hard to forgive; the burnt soup challenging the aroma of savoury pie from the staff hall; being called "silly goose" when, caught on the doorstep with my beau, I said goodnight after my first ball. I was clad in pink net and imagination, so that he was as dark, handsome and tall as Mr Rochester, instead of a pimply student from Trinity's divinity school. My face was so red and I felt such a fool that I cried all night in my bed.

How you must have missed the moor, as I miss the sea! Do they not know that wild flowers wither, and often die, when plucked from their lea?

Dear Charlotte and Emily, now I must end,
with love from me.

Jenny came to join me in my last year in Dublin.
She was only ten and Mother begged me to look
after her, which I willingly did, taking her part in
any sign of trouble or skirmish amongst the juniors.
She liked being in boarding school, probably because
she had me to champion her, and I sometimes
brought her with me when I took two or three
juniors for their daily walk or "down town" on a
Saturday morning. On one of these trips, a little girl
from far away in the west became enormously excited at the sight of pyramids of oranges and apples
outside fruit shops, and the fact that she thought
she only had to help herself posed a few problems for
me.

Then Father wrote that we had to come home, and
Jenny would have to go to Down High School. He
said that there was going to be a war, and he didn't
know where Éire would stand; the border might be
closed, Germany might get the southern ports and
we'd be marooned! Such dire predictions were new to
me. So politically unaware was I that I only knew
Hitler as the name of the principal's cat, which had
met a dreadful end when the cords of the old wooden
lift from the dining room broke and crashed down to
the kitchen to where poor Hitler was sleeping in the
lift shaft.

Jenny and I packed our belongings in an air of
importance, racing before the storm to come. Some
other northern girls who had elected to stay jeered

at us. I didn't mind leaving No 12 at all, but I felt sad about leaving Dublin. I wanted to go to Trinity. Belfast was, by comparison, unfamiliar, strange.

"Come home and think about it," Father wrote. "Jenny can't stay down there without you with the news of imminent war what it is."

I didn't understand. What war? Whose war?

# War and Engagement

FTER LEAVING COLLEGE in June, I found myself at a loss, confused not to be packing a trunk and catching a train from Belfast to Dublin. I was dying to go back. But life at the rectory wasn't good. Both of my parents were ill, Mother confined to bed, Father not able to take the services and dependent on help from other parishes, or from 'supply' clergy sent down from Belfast. I realised I'd have to stay at home and help out; it was too much for Philippa. Helen was still at school, a prefect, and playing important hockey matches for Ulster schools while studying for her senior. Robert was also still at school in Belfast, coming home only to be bored stiff with us all in the holidays, though one summer he found a girlfriend in the summer visitor's crowd and she brightened his horizon for him.

Amongst the 'supplies' sent down from Belfast to take the services were various curates whom Father thought would make good husbands for his daughters. Though he didn't really want to lose us, he felt that husbands of his choosing would mean a lesser loss, especially if they had parishes near by and we could be on hand. Such was his dependence. But we were adamant that we would not dream of marrying curates. We wanted lives comparable to those of the summer visitors: much more exciting, with elements of delightful risk and variety. One of the "supplies" took a fancy to Philippa, and after lunch one Sunday went with her into the shrubbery. Mother became anxious and sent me to join them. They were sitting in the grass under the orange blossom tree. It was very hot and the "supply" had removed his jacket and clerical collar, and he looked at me as though I were something repulsive. I wasn't enjoying myself either. Suddenly he scrabbled in the grass and, leaning towards me, dropped a small slippery frog down the front of my blouse. (I subsequently heard him preach several times during the years that followed and not a word penetrated my mind, transported as I was back to that summer garden and a wet green frog long ago.)

All that year, 1938, the rumblings of war went on. Father had his old crystal radio set with a large horn to which he listened, reporting to us the dire forebodings. We were not troubled by it then. We had enough to worry about trying to keep the rectory going and looking after both Mother and Father. He sat in his big horsehair chair in the dining room, near the door into Mother's room, relaying the news to her, complaining about the way we stayed out late, the way we dressed – 'provocative,' he said – until Mother grew weary of him and demanded that the door be shut. I felt sorry for them both, remembering the good companions they had been in our early days in Dunseverick.

In 1939 all father's gloomy predictions came true. I can still hear King George's sad voice announcing it, as I willed him not to stutter. Yet I couldn't accept that our lives were going to change all that much because of a war with the Germans. There seemed no reason why we should not go on enjoying ourselves, playing tennis, going out in boats with some of the fishermen, on hazardous, seasick journeys, then deciding that once was not enough. We swam at Lamb's Lough and Coney Island and went for long walks across the harbour at Ardtole, where there was the ruin of an old church with a violent history of a massacre at a Christmas midnight mass. It stood on a rise with wonderful views of the sea all around and had an eerie atmosphere when the sun was going down. We walked to Killough and, finding no excitement there, went on to St John's Point, and there before us was a magnificent view of the Mourne Mountains.

"They're away looking for fellas," Father told Mother glumly.

Mother was worried about Jenny. We didn't always want to take her with us on our jaunts, complaining unkindly that she was too young, too much of a nuisance. So she was often left to her own devices, until one day the postmistress reported to Father that his youngest daughter, aged just thirteen, had been seen sitting on the fish boxes on the harbour smoking. As if that weren't enough, she had also been seen travelling on the train to Downpatrick and meeting a young fellow at the pictures. Mother was in a state, especially after Father had roared his head off at Jenny in his anxiety and reduced her to a jelly. She never cried, but she was subdued for a while, and more careful about her clandestine movements.

"Look after her," Mother begged me tearfully, and I did my best.

We took the five shilling excursion train to Belfast most Thursdays and went to the Classic Cinema where there was a lovely cafe for afternoon tea, or to the Ritz to see Shirley Temple films. How we loved that dear little doll of a child star, with her round, faultless face and plump dancing ringlets! We relished a romantic Deanna Durban film full of her beautiful singing, and we fell in love with screen heroes like Gary Cooper, James Stewart and Clark Gable. I was in love with the English actor Lesley Howard in *The Scarlet Pimpernel* for years.

"Pack of eejits!" exploded Father when he heard us telling Mother about the films we had seen. Stuck in her bedroom, she listened to our excited, giggling accounts with wistful longing. She had always loved the theatre when she was in Dublin but had never been to a cinema.

"When you are well again, Mammy, you can come with us," we assured her, knowing full well that she would never walk again. Hadn't the doctor said so? Her legs were thin as sticks and twisted, her toes gangrenous. The rheumatoid arthritis had taken its toll, and no medicine did any good. But we had to keep her spirits up, and she still ran the house from her bed, continuing to do beautiful crochet and embroidery work until her hands failed her. We bought her a decent radio and she loved to listen to *Mrs Dale's Diary*, looking forward eagerly to each new instalment. Even in her illness, she provided a very important calm centre in our somewhat dishevelled lives.

Our jaunts to Belfast cost us a ten shilling note, which Father paid me for helping in the house, grumbling all the time that I'd have him in the poor house before long. Philippa was paid the same, and earned a little more for playing the organ in church on Sundays. Father had rallied a bit in health and was back in church and doing parochial visits again. I was disgusted at the waste of my education and decided I'd go to Belfast and get a job. But how to go about it? Then Father came up with a plan. I was astonished when he asked me if I'd like a job in Dublin.

"Not university?" I asked hopefully.

"You know I can't afford that," he said sadly, and I was sorry I'd asked. "No," he continued, "a job which would pay for digs and a bit over."

"What job?" I asked cautiously and hopefully together.

"In Guinness's brewery. You know I have a family connection."

I couldn't believe it. I remembered the all-pervading smell that emanated from the brewery all over the centre of Dublin, especially in the slums. I had thought it was a bakery smell, of bread being made for the Kylemore and all the little bakeries around the city. Then I had learned it was the yeast used in the brewing of beer, the thick Guinness my Mother didn't like when Father made her drink it for a tonic, and porter, pronounced 'porther' that was sent for in jugs under shawls and in prams and called a 'message' for respectability sake. Porter that made men into drunks, and women, too, lying about the streets with little children crying and clinging to them, little children that we pupils of a great and grand school used to gather into playgroups in a church hall and try to make their lives brighter, once a week. And my father, a clergyman, wanted me to earn my living perpetrating that!

I cheated. I went for the interview, determined to fail it, in order to have a day in my beloved Dublin. I answered the interviewer's questions reluctantly. She was a nice lady, an old Alexandran. Just my luck. She offered me the job. I hung my head, ashamed of my subterfuge, but determined. I declined, said I couldn't stand the smell. She said I'd get used to it. I got up to go, apologised for wasting her time, and found my way out. There was the smell of yeast again, and as I walked, almost ran, through the slums, my heart was glad that I'd had the courage to refuse when I saw the degradation of the poor who had no other source of ease from their situation than that awful 'porther'. After that I spent a lovely day in Dublin.

Father and I had a mighty row when the lady wrote to him from Guinness.

"You are altogether too high-minded for your own good," he roared at me. "Take care that you don't have a great fall some day."

"Maybe I'll join the women's forces," I retorted, the war for once coming to my aid.

"Indeed you will not. You'd only become a groundsheet for the army!"

"What's that?" I queried in my innocence. "Anyway, I prefer the air force, or even the navy. I like the navy uniform."

"Over my dead body!" he declared. "It's no life for a girl. If you want to help you can roll bandages for the Red Cross, or knit balaclavas."

There was to be a big Red Cross dance in Milligan's Hall in Ardglass and the excitement was great. Everybody would be going to support such an important cause. Except us, it seemed. Father wouldn't permit us to go without respectable partners.

"You are not going to be jostled about by all the locals, getting yourselves talked about."

He was cleaning his old gun while he spoke.

"For goodness sake," Mother exclaimed, "put that thing away. You scared the daylights out of poor drunk Sammy Duncan last night, shooting out of the bedroom window at him..."

"Over his head," Father laughed heartily. "What was he doing crashing around in our shrubbery? Might have been a German!"

"He'd only lost his way, mistaking our driveway for his own lane, and what on earth would a German be doing here, for goodness sake," she exclaimed again.

In despair about the dance, I suddenly thought of a plan that might work. I cornered Helen coming in one Saturday armed with her hockey stick, her cheeks pink with exercise and fresh air, her fair curls bouncing.

"Ask the English master, and the Latin master, at your school! Yes, yes," I was excited by my boldness and determined as her eyes opened in astonishment. "They're young. Ask them, and the science master too. Father can't have any objection to them as partners for us."

"I couldn't! I wouldn't have the nerve!" she protested.

"Yes, you can," I urged her. "You've told me how nice the English master is."

I nagged at her all week. I met her coming off the train.

"Have you asked them?"

"I'll ask tomorrow," she promised reluctantly.

"Otherwise we can't go, you know." I was insistent. "And it'll be such a grand affair. You want to go, too, don't you? Tomorrow's Friday and it's on Saturday!"

Helen nodded. "I'll ask tomorrow."

Mother was sympathetic to our efforts to meet young men and deplored her inability to help us.

On Friday a smiling Helen was able to announce proudly, very relieved.

"Yes, they're coming. 'Delighted,' they say, all three of them."

"That's marvellous," I cried, "one each!"

"Bags I the English master," she said.

"We'll see," I replied; "they have a choice too."

And that was how I met the English master, whose name was Ernest Maxwell.

Helen was quite happy with the science master, and Philippa with the Latin teacher. They called for us in Ernest's little old Morris car, which was a bit like a sewing machine, and somehow we all squeezed in. The dance was a great success, but I remember little of it, only Ernest's being there. Over the weeks that followed, Ernest's car chugged its way a few times between Ardglass and Downpatrick, and on our third date we got engaged. We celebrated the event in a milk bar in Belfast with Knicker-bocker Glories, the ring, a diamond cluster, winking on my finger.

Ernest was very good-looking, with dark hair and dark, searching eyes. He loved his subject, English, and taught it with all the enthusiasm he brought to everything he did. He was a graduate of Queen's University in Belfast, and once he took me around it, proudly showing it off to me. I was impressed but not as enthusiastic as he was, my preference being for Trinity in Dublin. He had been cox for the university rowing team, and president of the Literific Society in his last year; he wrote poetry and read the poems to me, which I loved.

"You'll be in print some day," I assured him.

# A Dream of Wonderland

IT WAS WONDERFUL to be engaged. I was nineteen and I flashed the ring all over Ardglass and Downpatrick. Everybody seemed glad for me, though my parents were surprised, bewildered in a way at first, then thankful. Here, after all, was an eminently suitable young man wanting to marry their unpredictable, basically bolshevik eldest daughter; they could find no fault in him. They bought me new clothes for going to meet his people in Belfast, and Mother suggested that I should go to the hairdresser.

"But why?" I cried. "Ernest likes me the way I am!"

Father found a new audience in Ernest. Having been a teacher in his young days in Dublin, he found a lot in common with Ernest, and they talked and talked until I had to drag my fiancé out to get his attention.

"You're a lucky girl," Father told me. "He's a fine fellow, for all that he's a Presbyterian."

"What's wrong with them?" I asked in protest. "They're Christians, same as we are!"

I'd asked the same question years before about Catholics, and I think Father enjoyed an easier rapport with Catholics than with Presbyterians.

"Oh nothing," Father answered hurriedly, "they're

grand people, very upright, worthy. You'll have to mind your p's and q's!"

I left him in disgust.

I had by this time got a job as a secretary in Downpatrick. As Ernest had digs in Downpatrick, he came for me in the afternoons and saw me on to the train for Ardglass, sometimes coming with me, but more regularly visiting me in his funny little car. When it let us down, we used our bicycles, Ernest borrowing Father's big old one with the saddlebag that was so useful for carrying a picnic. We picnicked all over Lecale, up and down the Quoile River. Sometimes we sailed down the river to Strangford Lough when Ernest could borrow his cousin's boat. He loved sailing. I had romantic notions about lying back on cushions like the young men and girls on the River Cam I had seen in films, but this was different. I had to work in this boat: grab this line, furl that, furl this, move over, this side then that. But I loved Strangford Lough and the Quoile River the way Ernest did.

"Some day I'll buy a boat of my own," he declared, "and we'll sail all over the lough and out to sea. We'll buy a house by the lough and come back to it from wherever we are. What do you say?"

I hugged him hard, his dream mine.

One day we rode our bicycles, taking a picnic in the saddlebag, to Ballyhornan. It was a favourite place, with a clean strand and an island, called Gun's Island.

"I wonder if it is called after a man named Gun, or does it refer to guns smuggled in to use in some of the troubles," I surmised.

*Gun's Island*

We waited for low tide, left our bicycles on the strand and walked across to the island. Nobody lived on it, though there was a ruined cottage where cattle sheltered while other cattle roamed free. They were timid and ran away from us. The grass was thick, silky and green and full of wild flowers. The hedges were white now in May with hawthorn.

"This island is ours today," I exclaimed. "There's no one else about." We walked around it, spread our picnic on a flat rock on the sea side of the island, lay in the bracken and gazed at the far pale blue line of horizon.

"Nothing between us and Scotland. D'you think your cousin's boat would make it?" I teased.

We forgot the time, and the tide. When we reached the home side of the island, the tide was fast flowing in and we were surrounded. Our bicycles lay on the sand, being washed by the incoming wavelets.

"They'll soon be afloat," I cried.

"Come on, we'll have to swim for it." Ernest grabbed my hand and pulled me down to the water.

"Sure, you know I can't swim!" I yelled.

"It's not deep yet; hold on to me;" and he plunged in.

It wasn't deep and we were able to wade ashore, but we were soaked to the skin. We picked up our bicycles and wheeled them up to the road.

It had been a warm day, but now it was getting cool as we rode along in our wet clothes. Mine were light and they dried quickly on me in the little breeze I created, but I shivered nevertheless. Ernest's trousers were still dripping salt water.

128

"I thought you knew about tides," he exclaimed, "living by the sea as you do."

"You didn't think about the time," I retorted. "I'm going to get a bad chill out of this."

"Nothing to what I'll suffer. I can feel a chest cold coming on," Ernest grumbled.

By the time we reached Ardglass we had fallen out completely. I went off to try and get a hot bath, if the heat in the coal range was enough, and Father drove Ernest back to Downpatrick to where his landlady fussed over him.

"She saved me from catching my death of a cold," Ernest said resentfully the next day when we met after school.

"I'm going to be a very bad wife." I hung my head.

He relented, and we both burst into laughter.

"Your father gave me a hot toddy that really did the trick," he said, "and nothing could ever spoil that lovely day on the island, could it?"

Another day when my sister Helen and Ernest's brother were with us, we were caught in a sudden squall in Strangford Lough in Ernest's cousin's boat. Putting in at an island where Ernest had a tent, we moored the boat safely and the four of us lay on a ground sheet with a tarpaulin over us and laughed at the storm, snug and safe with never an uncomfortable thought between us. Ernest had beer in the boat and dashed out in a lull in the storm to get it. I had a flask of tea and a parcel of sandwiches, but had forgotten cups, so when the beer was finished we drank our tea out of the beer cans. It had never tasted so good. Ernest's brother found a copy of

*On Strangford Lough*

Plato's *Republic* in a wooden box Ernest kept in the boat and brought it to the tent. He began to read it to us without any punctuation, and soon he had us laughing uproariously and irreverently at this august work.

When the storm died down, the lough was so calm that we had trouble getting the boat going. Ernest had us capering about it from side to side, bow to stern, the sail billowing fitfully, in an effort to catch what little wind there was. He was so serious about it that we laughed at him.

"Earnest Ernest!" we called, flapping about in the boat to his commands.

But his skippering brought us safely ashore, where we beached and moored the boat and set off for home in his little car. The sun was shining now, the sky piled high with swiftly moving white clouds, and we could see in the distance the monkey puzzle tree in our garden in Ardglass. I was reminded of a passage in one of my childhood books, *Alice's Adventures in Wonderland*: "how she would keep, through all her riper years... a dream of Wonderland of long ago, and feel the simple joys, remembering... the happy summer days."

# The War

THE REALITY OF the war struck home to me when one day Ernest came and told me that he had joined up in the RAF. I was astonished.

"But why?" I cried. "There's no need. It's not our war!"

"You've been too long in Dublin," he smiled. "It is indeed our war. I have to go. The boys in my class are impatient to reach the age when they can go. I can't leave it all to them."

"What about me? And your job? What about us?" I was indignant.

"The job will wait, and you, will you wait for me?"

I hung my head to hide my tears.

"Of course I will, but it's not fair!"

"War is never fair," he said, lifting my chin. "You're so – so – ungrown up! I think I'll call you Alana, the way your mother does."

"Alana Maxwell," I brightened, "that sounds nice. "But – but – it means 'child' in Irish. I suppose you think I'm childish now. It was that boarding school did it to me, arrested my development, I expect."

"Don't take it so seriously," he laughed, "and don't lose it all anyway. You are who you are, and I love you that way."

I was comforted for the time being, but became increasingly incensed by the war as it loomed closer.

Ernest's parents lived in a large red-brick house, the manse, near their church in Belfast, and I found them both, but especially his mother, very easy to get on with. They must have felt that Ernest meant business when he brought me to meet them for the first time, for they did look me over. Although I sensed their particular interest, they made me most welcome, and always afterwards they were kind and helpful. I noticed how like his mother Ernest was, with the same dark, searching eyes, though she was a big woman and he was slender and only medium tall.

They had a funny little black and white dog of nondescript pedigree called Gyp; he was really Ernest's dog but lived in the manse and was treated like a human being, given every consideration without being in any way spoiled. He reciprocated with affectionate friendliness, and was much nicer than most human beings.

During the war Ernest's parents had a concrete Anderson air raid shelter installed in their kitchen which took up most of the room. When the air raid siren sounded, Gyp would be first into the shelter, followed by an old lady who lived a little way down the road, armed with her knitting. She didn't belong to the congregation and she never spoke a word, but she was expected and allowed in every time. This meant that if Ernest and his brother were at home, they had to crouch under the stairs during an air raid, as the shelter held only four, or five at a pinch, and the old lady was very large.

Ernest went away soon after joining up, to be trained somewhere in England as a pilot.

"Ah ha!" I exclaimed. "You want to learn to fly! That's why you're going."

"That as well," he replied. "You know I've always been keen, but now this gives me the opportunity."

My brother left school as soon as he reached the age and joined the RAF too. He came home from abroad after long intervals away and sat on Mother's bed as he had done when he came home from school, telling her all about his life in the RAF. Her tired, sad eyes lit up as she listened avidly. We had long ago given up teasing this stranger brother who came and went from school and the Forces, now grown up and handsome in his blue uniform. But he was never a stranger to his mother.

Many of the local young men went into the army and navy and were sent all over the world. For many it was an adventure, a chance to get away from home, to see the world, to learn a trade.

For us at home it meant ration books, gas masks, shortages. As I stood in a queue for onions, they ran out just as the woman before me held out her money and coupons, and she burst into tears. She was at her wits end, she cried, trying to make tasty meals for her family, and the chance of onions was hard to miss. The man before her shared his with her.

We were all encouraged to grow what we could, and land was made available for plots in the towns and in the city. Our coupons covered basics, but food was monotonous and plain. We made a "banana" spread out of parsnips, a little sugar and banana flavouring. It was an awful concoction, as was dried egg omelette, especially without onions.

We had potatoes and cabbages in the garden and children got free orange juice and Virol. Nobody starved, but we were bored with food the way it was. Trips over the border to bring back a pound of butter, a bit of chocolate or a round of beef became exciting, and we were lucky if we didn't have to hand the whole lot over to the customs officials. Many with sympathetic feelings turned a blind eye. Nylon stockings were another matter and were confiscated immediately.

On one occasion a priest coming up from a visit to Dublin was asked if he had anything to declare in his case.

"A whole clatter of nylon stockings!" he answered cheerfully.

"Och, away wi' ye, Father," the customs officer replied and passed him through.

The priest delightedly regaled his grateful lady parishioners with the story as he distributed the nylons amongst them.

My father loved funny stories arising from the wartime conditions, for they lightened the atmosphere created by the daily radio bulletins of disaster and continuing German advance. His favourite was of a wee fellow perched on his backyard fence shooting his toy pistol at the German planes flying over Belfast, and his mother shouting at him, "Come in out o' that and stop aggravatin' them!"

At the time of the dreadful Belfast Blitz, fire fighters from over the border came to our aid. A casualty awoke from being blown into unconsciousness to hear the southern accent of one of these firemen and exclaimed, "By God, that must have been a bloody big bomb to blow me all the way to Dublin!"

Stories like these made us laugh, often even immoderately, a relief from the solemn news bulletins.

"You'd better forget about French and brush up on your German," suggested Father more than once. "We're done for."

He was very gloomy, due to high blood pressure in part at least, but I constantly reminded him about defeatist talk. He responded by giving out about de Valera and the southern ports.

"Drat the man!" he'd explode. "Neutrality indeed! If the Germans invade us, it's a short march from Belfast Lough to Dublin! Then they'll know who's the boss!"

"Careless talk costs lives," I reminded him and, knowing that I was worried about Ernest, he would desist.

Ersatz was the "in" word, and we had ersatz coffee and ersatz jam. Four ounces of butter had to last a week. We made black-out curtains, so that no lights would show to guide the German airforce to targets in Belfast. The black-out material required no coupons and was a boon to those who liked to wear black skirts and evening dresses, even providing the makings of wee boys' school trousers.

We could hear the different "thrumm, thrumm," of the German engines going over, and I experienced the awful feeling that someone was out to get us. There were posters everywhere advising that careless talk costs lives, but they didn't stop rumours. In

Ardglass the friendly, trusting atmosphere changed. If an unfamiliar ship appeared on the horizon or something that looked like a submarine, tongues wagged. Who was in league with the enemy? Weren't the nationalists up the Falls Road lighting the Germans to the shipyards? Then the Blitz came in April 1941, and after that there was no more trouble about black-outs. It seemed the Germans didn't know the difference between the Shankill and the Falls. They missed the shipyards and dropped their bombs all over the city indiscriminately, and there were more civilians killed in that first raid than in any other city in England. We in little unimportant Ardglass cowered, and were thankful when the planes passed over us.

Then evacuees came from Belfast. Because of Mother's illness, we didn't have to have any, but church halls and schools were utilised. They camped in corridors and classrooms like gypsies, but got so bored they departed back to Belfast as soon as the coast was clear. Down High School was fumigated after them.

British soldiers were billeted in King's Castle, which was no longer a restaurant, and they nearly blew it and themselves up in an explosion in their arms room. After the British came the Americans, who had the castle all done up for themselves and sent pictures home to show the folks the grandeur they were living in. They really believed Ardglass was the sticks and spent their spare time trying to make libertines of the local girls. The description, current at that time, of their being "over-paid, over-

sexed and over here" seemed to fit. With uniforms
tailored to perfection, their peaked caps worn at an
angle, their pockets full of dollars, they were the
poor Irish girl's answer to Clark Gable.

Nevertheless, in spite of Father and the double-
barrelled shot-gun, Philippa met a nice chap from
Kentucky called Virgil. We were impressed by the
name, and when he came to church Father invited
him to the rectory.

"Come and tell me about yourself, Virgil."

When Virgil invited Philippa to a dance in
Killough, an officers' do, she made herself an
evening dress out of a white lace curtain, for which
no coupons were needed, and lined it with some soft
pink silk Mother had left from baby dresses. It was
most most attractive, and she looked beautiful. She
had grown tall and boasted long thick brown hair,
dark brown eyes and the looks of a Hedy Lamarr. It
was no wonder that Virgil was in love with her, for
we were sure that he was, and she with him.

But everything went wrong on the night of the
dance. She had not arrived home by midnight,
despite Father's stipulation that she should, which
had prompted Virgil, laughing, to call her
Cinderella. Father was very angry and Mother dis-
played a state of anxiety to match his own. All night
neither of them could sleep, even though I assured
them that such army functions did invariably continue long into the night.

She arrived home finally on the five o'clock milk
train, just herself and the driver and the milk bot-
tles in crates for the Ardglass market. Virgil had had

to go on duty and had put her on the train himself at Killough.

When she got off at Ardglass station, the driver looked at her. "What do you think you're doing at this time of the morning in your nightdress?"

"It's not a nightdress," Philippa exclaimed indignantly, "it's an evening dress. I've been dancing all night."

"Aye, I believe you, but will your father?"

At the mention of Father, Philippa trembled, then gathered up her skirts and walked up the hill and home.

"I thought Virgil was an officer and a gentleman!" Father roared, his face purple with anger, blood pressure and anxiety.

"It wasn't his fault," pleaded Philippa. "I wanted to stay on. I was having such a good time. He did remind me at 12 o'clock, but I wanted to stay."

Next day Virgil came and apologised to Father and Mother and they were mollified. He was good-looking, well-mannered and well-educated.

Then Virgil was sent away to North Africa. Philippa gave him a little pair of earrings as a keepsake and wrote to him. He wrote back several times, and then the letters stopped. Philippa heard no more until a letter came from America. It was from his mother. Virgil had been killed in North Africa. His mother told Philippa that she had found her letters to her son and the earrings, and knew that they had loved each other. Philippa wrote back and a correspondence developed which later resulted in an invitation to Kentucky and the fare to take her there. Mother thought it a great chance for her. Like so many Irish mothers, she viewed America as the land to which children emigrated, believing the grass was greener, their chances of a good life greater. All the same, she wept bitter tears, declaring that she would never see her again.

I went with Philippa to Shannon airport to see her off. Here she met another girl going out in similar hopes and was excited and happy at the prospect of this adventure. I stood on the airport tarmac until she disappeared, witnessing many other goodbyes and the tears and anguish on other faces. But Philippa never looked back and we would have lost her from the family had I not been an inveterate letter writer and kept in touch. It was twenty-five years before her feet touched Irish soil again, and by then Mother had died.

# Rostrevor, 1941

ERNEST RANG UP from somewhere abroad and asked me to marry him the following week when he was due for a week's leave.

"Yes, of course," I said, but then I succumbed to a sudden state of panic. How was I to be ready in one week? I wanted a trousseau, a bottom drawer, a white dress with a train, bridesmaids, and the whole parish invited!

"It wouldn't be appropriate in wartime, Alana," Mother assured me. "We wouldn't have enough coupons. You can have mine for a nice dress length and you can make it yourself."

In the event I did just that, and the resulting blue cloqué dress was pronounced beautiful. I managed to scrounge a few more clothing coupons from the family and friends and made another dress and a glamorous nightdress for my honeymoon.

Our combined food coupons allowed Philippa to make an iced fruit cake, sausage rolls and egg sandwiches – the eggs from our own hens – apple tart – again our own apples – and real sherry from Dublin for the cake. Uncle Herbert, Auntie May's cello-playing husband from Dun Laoghaire, came to give me away, and as he was a teetotaller he wouldn't even taste the wedding cake and had to have extra apple tart instead. Sadly, Mother was unable to come to the church, but from her wheel-chair at home she enjoyed the reception.

Knowing nothing about wedding etiquette, we did everything spontaneously, and the result was a lovely, simple, never-to-be-forgotten day. Ernest and his best man had come straight from an RAF station the day before and he hadn't a clean shirt. I washed one for him, dried it on the boiler and ironed it early on the morning of the wedding. My father and Ernest's, the two clergymen, both married us, pronouncing the blessing together. Helen, my brides-maid, also wore blue and looked delightful. I thought that the best man – another pilot, who rejoiced in the romantic name of Quentin – might like Helen, and they did get on well on the day, but after the wedding he was sent away overseas, and we never saw him again; he was lovely and lost to us.

At the reception Auntie May took photographs in the garden with her Brownie camera, and after-wards we left for Belfast in a taxi and from there continued by train to the seaside town of Rostrevor.

It lay beyond the Mourne Mountains, a beautiful little place at the head of Carlingford Lough, and Ernest had booked us into the Great Northern Railway hotel for two days and night. To me, unused to hotels, it was sumptuous and, nestling against a steep wooded hill, it had a superb view over the lough to Omeath and the Carlingford Mountains across the border in Eire. The lough was busy, small ships and fishing boats sailing up and down, with a big British navy ship at the mouth keeping a watch over all.

The staff at the hotel were kind and friendly, and I thought that the special attention they gave us meant that they had guessed we were newly married, even though, shy about it, I had carefully brushed any confetti from our clothes. Then I noticed the deference they afforded my husband, their open admiration as they looked at the pilot's wings on his blue tunic. He was handsome, this husband of mine.

Husband! Mine! I could hardly believe it. I linked his arm proudly and possessively as we followed the porter with our two overnight cases up the wide staircase to our room. Again it was sumptuous, with its big double bed, from which I quickly averted my eyes, polished mahogany wardrobe and dressing table, a wide window overlooking the lough with two comfortable chairs beside it.

Before going down to dinner, we unpacked our toiletries and night things, the white satin and lace nightdress I had made spilling over the bed. I hurriedly gathered it up and put it in under the pillow. Ernest left blue pyjamas on the bed while he went to the bathroom. We had hardly exchanged a word. I wandered to the window. Dusk was falling and lights were coming on over the border. On our side the black-out was in force, and I could just see silent shapes moving up and down the lough, the minimum lights for safety flickering here and there.

Ernest came back and held out his hand. "Come on; dinner," he said. "I'm hungry."

Relaxing, I took his hand and together we ran downstairs to the dining room. There a table set in the window was waiting for us and a pleasant grey-haired waiter gave us his full attention.

"My son is in the air force too, sir," he said as he took our orders.

The two men chatted for a moment while I looked around the room. There were a few elderly residents, some army men with their wives or girlfriends, and several naval officers. Ernest was the only air force officer, which perhaps accounted for the attention we were getting.

The waiter addressed me as "madam", which startled me at first. Dinner was delicious and plentiful in spite of rationing; when we remarked on this, the waiter winked and indicated the lights of Éire across the water.

"A little help from our friends goes a long way," he whispered.

After dinner we went for a walk into the little town. A moon had risen and gave us a clear light, all others quenched. There was very little traffic. All was quiet, yet with that air of tension prevalent everywhere during the war. We walked by the sea wall, watching the silent ships with their subdued lighting slide through the waves on our side of the lough. Now and then a brightly lit one would put out from the other side or come from the sea, merchant ships on their way up the canal to Newry and Warrenpoint.

On our return to the hotel, we were offered a drink: "on the house" the manager said as he brought it to us in the lounge. I had sherry, the only drink I was familiar with, and Ernest had a brandy.

How we enjoyed sitting there being fêted! We sat for ages, not talking much, watching the lough from the dimly lit room until the curtains were fully drawn and no lights shone outside.

When we eventually entered our bedroom, we found it full of moonlight, the moon above the mountains shining straight in the windows.

We sat in the comfortable chairs and feasted on the loveliness, hands held, quiet, and a little nervous.

"I'm tired," Ernest announced suddenly. "It's been an exhausting day."

He got up, took his pyjamas from the bed and went to the bathroom. I hurriedly slipped out of my clothes and into my white satin finery.

"Draw the curtains," Ernest spoke from the bed, "before I switch on this light."

I started to draw them, slowly, shivering a little. They were green brocade with a pattern of vine leaves, gold-threaded and heavily embroidered.

"You'll certainly remember that pattern for a long while," Ernest suggested in an amused voice.

I quickly closed the curtains tight and, turning, saw where he had hung his jacket on a chair. My fingers gently caressed the silver thread of the wings glinting in the soft bedside light.

I was as happy then as I would ever be, feeling that my world was now complete.

# Parting

As soon as we returned from our honeymoon,
Ernest was suddenly sent abroad. I went to
the railway station to see him off to the boat
at Larne. There were many other goodbyes being
said, and ours were unnoticed and private amongst
the many. Ernest gave me a poem he had written.

"Read it later, somewhere where you and I have
been and loved," he said.

The train's piercing whistle startled us, and I drew
back on the station platform as the train moved off.
Only then did I notice that the uniforms had all gone
and the platform held only women in tears. We all
stood in silence until the train, men still hanging out
of the windows waving, was out of sight.

I walked dazedly to a seat in the station, sat down
and cried. As I dried my eyes on my ball of white
handkerchief, I became aware of an army man sitting beside me, grinning at me.

"That's right, luv," he said. "There's more fish in
the sea!"

I stared at him, unbelieving.

"What about it, luv? The air force can't have all
the pretty girls. What about the bleedin' army, eh?"

I stood up, my anger making me haughty. "How
dare you! That was my husband!"

The man grinned again at me. "So what? There's a

war on! Bet there's plenty of WAFs to keep him warm!"

"You pig!" I screamed, and raised my hand.

A military policeman walked towards us. "You annoying this lady?" he asked the army man coolly.

"Bloody stuck-up air force bitch!" I heard the man reply as I began to run. I ran through a throng of people, and then suddenly there was a girl I knew. I grabbed her and burst into further tears.

"Pat! I'm so glad to see you."

She looked at me, untangled my arms. "You look very pale. Come for a coffee."

We went to a cafe across the street, and I welcomed the warm cup, hugging it with my hands.

"How did you come to be here?" I asked Pat.

"I was seeing an army fellow off. I met him at a dance last night. He comes from Scotland and hadn't anyone to see him off."

"You are such a softy, Pat." I couldn't help smiling.

"It's lonely for a fellow not to have someone to see him off. No harm done. There seems to be something big on."

"And I had a fight with a fellow who made a pass at me! I nearly hit him. I could have been kinder."

"Anyway, how'd the honeymoon go?"

This made me cry again, for our two days had seemed such a cruelly short time.

"God, you didn't get a chance!"

She took my hand.

"It's just that I was looking forward to it so much, having him to myself for twenty-four hours a day, for a while. D'you know, Pat, from what I've seen of marriages, these first days are the only time both people *want* to be together for twenty-four hours a day. So they're precious. Oh, why did it have to happen!"

"Why did it?" Pat asked.

"As you said, something big on, a flap as they say in the air force. It frightens me."

Ernest was sent to South Africa to a place called Bulawayo, and from there he sent letters telling me how much he liked it and how maybe we would spend a part of our lives there. He'd get a job teaching English after the war and we would see a bit of the world together.

"Bulawayo is beautiful," he wrote.

"I'll go anywhere with you," I replied, "but don't forget Strangford Lough."

"Oh, that's for our retirement," he replied with youthful enthusiasm. He was twenty-five.

The war rolled on with its shortages and blackouts and yellow telegrams from the War Office invading homes with "We regret to inform you... killed... prisoner of war... missing, believed killed." Three of my friends received these telegrams.

Then Ernest came home and we had a few days – scarcely a week – together, before he was sent to Ballykelly, where he flew the giant American Flying Fortress planes, and where I was able to join him. He found a flat for us and I felt really married at last. For two months I was able to enjoy a bit of fun there on the station with other young wives. When Ernest, who was now in Bomber Command, went out on a sortie, he used to dip his plane for me as he flew over the little town of Limavady. I was so proud as I saw those beautiful white machines, like enormous seagulls, flying over and knew that the middle leading plane, dipping slightly as though in a graceful bow, was flown by my husband.

Soon after this brief interlude of married life, Ernest was sent to Cranwell in England to train young pilots. One night his crew were playing cards. He was due to take a Wellington bomber up the next day with a trainee pilot and suddenly decided to give it a test run. Not wanting to interrupt the card game, he took just his observer, a young chap from New Zealand, with him. The plane developed a fault on the run in and crashed on the station, bursting into flames. They were both killed.

The telegram came on a Sunday, just before church, while I was in Belfast with his parents. My father-in-law, the minister, sent the assistant minister to take the service in his stead, and turned to us, Ernest's mother and me, the telegram rustling in his shaking hand.

# Epilogue

FATHER BECAME THE victim of a massive stroke and we had to leave our beloved home, which belonged to the church. We moved to an old house in Belfast, a tall, grim terrace house, which was all our meagre resources would allow. We would rather have stayed in Ardglass or Downpatrick, but we all had to get jobs and help out as Father was too young to have accumulated much of a pension from the church. So Belfast it had to be. Soon after we moved, father died, aged fifty-seven.

He had been sitting in Mother's room, talking to her about the old days and his childhood, she had only been half listening, when suddenly he said, "I think I'll go home."

"Home?" she queried. "Sure this is home now. Do you mean Ardglass?"

"No, Dublin," he said slowly, and he smiled. "I'd like to go home to Dalkey."

Then he mumbled something else, his head fell forward and he stiffened as if in pain.

We raced for the local doctor who lived in the same terrace. He injected something and asked if we wanted him sent to a nursing home.

We said we could not afford a nursing home, so he was taken to the Royal Victoria, where, no beds being available, he died on a trolley in a corridor.

Helen married a Belfast man, and later Jenny did too. In the meantime the war had ended, and restrictions were eased. Both Helen and Jenny had white weddings, a proper reception in a hotel and at least a week's honeymoon, returning to their own houses. I thought of the short time I'd had with Ernest and was glad for them.

Robert came home from India, where he had been with the RAF, demobilised and looking for a job. He stayed with Mother and me for a while, went into the civil service, then married a Belfast girl, and they found a home of their own.

All these events hurried us through the years until there were only Mother and me left. I'd preferred to hurry along through weddings, funerals, departures alike, leaving thinking about them for tomorrow. They hurt too much to dwell upon today.

Now Mother and I looked at each other, both of us widows. I was in my twenties; she was in her fifties. Each of us had pensions and I had a part-time job. We thought we could manage quietly and keep each other company, maybe dispel the loneliness, in part anyway.

A visitor from Ardglass told us that the rectory there was to be demolished, since it had been discovered that there was something wrong with the foundations, and a bungalow was to be erected in its place. We were horrified to think that that beautiful historic old house, surely a planter's original, was to be pulled down, and I arranged to take a sentimental journey down to Ardglass to bid it farewell.

I walked from the railway station up the familiar

hill, along past the national school, and there stood the house, denuded of its lovely rich ivy. The garden lay untended, the monkey puzzle had gone, and the whole site was just waiting for the bulldozers. Their tracks had already churned up the gravel, and a glass pane in the porch was broken.

Sadly I turned away. I took the road down to the church, pushed open the door and went inside. Sitting there in the quietness in what used to be the rectory pew, I could hear my father's voice in the prayer he had used so often at evening prayer.

"May He support us all the day long till the shades lengthen and the evening comes, and the busy world is hushed and the fever of life is over and our work is done; then in His mercy may He give us safe" – and here he always changed the word lodging, for the fishermen and those who depended on them – "safe harbour and a holy rest and peace at the last!"

The afternoon sunshine was casting stripes of light and shadow across the aisle as I left.

I walked over the golf links and sat on a rock looking out to sea, where Ernest and I had sat and talked many times. I opened my handbag and took out one of his letters to me. Idling through it I found the lines: "When I come home we will talk about so many things, sometimes with friends, but mostly to each other. Remember 'Heraclitus'*: 'I wept, as I remembered, how often you and I had tired the sun with talking and sent him down the sky.'"

*William Cory: "Heraclitus", translation of Callimachus, *Epigrams*, 2.

And I wept, too, for the loss of my love to talk to and to talk to me.

Then I read the poem he had written especially for me.

### Sonnet

To see the Spring awake once more the sky;
Once more to feel the everflowing beat
Of life renewed in soil and sea! The cry
Of wheeling gulls, the strong pull of the sheet
On days of cloud and foam, when strange,
   immense
In power, the dense seas stir: these things
My mind long winter-bound awake, my sense
Release from a half-life; yet still there springs
A dread, lest by a sharper winter's tooth
We may, by fortune's or by war's despite,
Be doomed to lose those welcomers of youth
And freeze in deserts reft of earth's delight.
You only left, in these depth's triumphing,
We still shall make our own diviner Spring.

Flying Officer Ernest Maxwell, RAF
Killed in action, February 1943

# Also published by Brandon

**Vivienne Draper**
*The Children of Dunseverick*

Her enchanting first book, an evocative account of a childhood spent in an old rectory on the north coast of Antrim.

"It is the tone of the book which most engages, the unmistakable presence of tolerant humanity. The proof is in the pudding indeed, as Ms Draper does justice to her rearing. A worthy and delightful read."
*The Irish Times*

"Vivienne Draper's memories will evoke many a responsive chord. She has woven a shining necklace of tales, and so fresh and immediate is the writing that the reader is at once drawn back into her varnished world of the 1920's in all its simplicity and charm." *Linen Hall Review*

*ISBN 0 86322 195 5; 160 pages, illustrated paperback; £6.95*

## Alice Taylor

### *To School Through the Fields*
"Taylor's telling makes the world of her village univer-sal, and sets her firmly in that mysteriously potent Irish storytelling tradition." *Los Angeles Times*
*ISBN 0 86322 099 1; 160 pages; paperback £5.99*

### *Quench the Lamp*
"Infused with wit and lyricism, the story centers on the 1950s when the author and her friends were budding teenagers." *Publishers Weekly*
*ISBN 0 86322 112 2; 160 pages; paperback £5.99*

### *The Village*
"She has a wicked wit and a pen which works on the reader slowly but insidiously." *Observer*
*ISBN 0 86322 142 4; 160 pages; paperback £5.99*

### *Country Days*
"A rich patchwork of tales and reminiscences by the bestselling village postmistress from Co. Cork. Alice Taylor is a natural writer." *Daily Telegraph*
*ISBN 0 86322 168 8; 160 pages; paperback £5.99*

### *The Night Before Christmas*
"A nostalgic and loving look back to a family firmly rooted in tradition and humour... It truly pulls back the curtain of time to the days when Christmas was really Christmas." *Examiner*
*ISBN 0 86322 138 6; 160 pages, paperback; £5.95*

# *Holidays*

As TERM NEARED its end, the prospect of going home for the holidays ushered in a wonderful and exciting period of anticipation. However, I was finding that going home only three times a year was isolating me in part from my family, and also from my community. Robert found this, too, and he complained that his sisters were becoming strangers to him. We for our part decided he was too much of a stranger to impose silly tricks upon and so we stopped the teasing with which we used to plague him. Since his school friends had scattered to their homes across the province, he found the holidays lonely and trying. Except for sitting on Mother's bed and telling her all about his separate life at school, he had nothing to do except wander down to the harbour and watch the fishing boats and their crews. He always cheered up when the end of the holidays came and Father drove him up to Belfast and school again.

I, too, found that I was often lonely in the holidays. Philippa and Helen had friends at school in Downpatrick and the surrounding countryside and were often invited out. Helen played hockey for the school and latterly for Ulster, so was fully occupied with important matches. Philippa devoted most of her time to golf and to playing the organ in church.

She had been unhappy at school and Father had let her leave; after all, he needed her at home to help him look after Mother. Mary hadn't been replaced when she married her boyfriend, and the rectory had become a sad and neglected house. Jenny, returning home from school, would find nobody in except Mother, chained to her bed, impotent and unhappy. Jenny would make her a cup of tea and herself a slice of bread and jam, and then Philippa, coming in from golf, would get the evening meal ready. She was kind and gentle with Mother, and the evenings when we were all in the house seemed brighter.

But I noticed differences every time I came home. Father wasn't well himself; he was often "taking turns", Mother said, and eating far too much: "comfort eating" she called it. "He has so much to worry about: me in this helpless state, the two parishes to look after. The doctor says his heart isn't too good, but he won't listen to the doctor."

I found that he had become more irascible and dogmatic than before.

"If I say the moon is made of green cheese, it is made of green cheese!" He shouted at us.

The unfortunate result of his bad temper was that none of us took anything he said seriously. Rows and arguments ensued. We were growing up and he couldn't accept it. He had become paranoid about boyfriends, Philippa and Helen said. They knew several boys about the place and were both very pretty. I could only envy them. I had no boyfriend. Where would I meet one, after all, incarcerated as I was in a female institution.

"When I leave Dublin, I'll marry the first man who asks me!" I threatened Father.

He laughed: "Get thee to thy nunnery, girl!"

My sisters complained, to my envious queries, that it was no fun having boyfriends. They said Father would be hovering about the garden with the double-barrelled gun he'd had for shooting rabbits in Dunseverick. He'd say now that he was shooting at crows, but the boys, not too sure of his aim, beat a hasty retreat yards before the rectory gate.

Nevertheless, one evening Helen and Philippa were allowed to bring boyfriends home, Mother having said it was best to see how they'd behave as guests in the house. The drawing room fire was lit, the piano was dusted and supper was laid, but when the boys were ensconced in easy chairs, in came Father, who loved an audience, and who launched into a series of long stories of Dublin, his life as a teacher and many a tall tale culled from the various parishes he had served in. Philippa and Helen had heard them all and were not amused. One of them went to Mother.

"What'll we do? How will we get him out?"

"Tell him I want him," Mother said, and she did her best to keep him with her on some pretext or other. Inevitably, however, he came back to the drawing room and resumed his monologue. Further visits of boyfriends followed and further attempts were made to prevent Father monopolising proceedings, and sometimes desperate remedies were employed. One night after three hours of endless talk out of him, Philippa went out into the haggard and pulled up the stakes which tethered his two goats.

"Dad, the goats are loose!" she exclaimed on her return.

Fussing and fuming, Father hurried after them, but by now they were several fields away and reluctant to surrender their newly acquired freedom. As Father chased them outside, the evening continued inside as planned until 11 o'clock, Mother's deadline, which Philippa conveyed none too subtly by playing the National Anthem to signal that it was time for the boys to be going home. As Father had rounded up the goats by that time, he was not grudged a few minutes' chat as the guests were leaving.

The existence of boyfriends was now tolerated, but we were not encouraged to have Catholic boyfriends.

As I had my eye on a very good-looking young Catholic fellow in the village, I asked belligerently, "Why not? They're Christians, same as we are!"

"Marriage is a difficult enough estate to enter into without making it more so by marrying out of your own kind. I assure you, they wouldn't like it any more than I would," Father replied.

Once when we had newly arrived in Ardglass, Father had been driving along with us, the four girls, in the car when we had stopped to talk to a Catholic teacher whom he knew. As their conversation had drawn to a close, the man had looked at us and asked, "Will they be growing up in Ardglass, will ye tell me?"

When Father had nodded, he had answered firmly, "I'm off to lock up my sons!"

604 **Liberian Historical Review.**
Monrovia: Liberian Historical Society, 1964-1972. annual.
Published annually in Monrovia by the Liberian Historical Society for almost a decade, this publication now appears to be discontinued. Amongst its editors and contributors were some of Liberia's leading scholars, who analysed in many interesting articles the more important issues in Liberian history.

605 **Liberian Studies Journal.**
Sewanee, Tennessee: University of the South (since 1985), 1968- . biannual.
A publication of the Liberian Studies Association, a scholarly body incorporated in the United States, the *Liberian Studies Journal* (LSJ) is a refereed journal that focuses primarily on the social sciences and the humanities and is 'devoted to studies of Africa's oldest republic'. The LSJ is perhaps the only 'continuous scholarly' journal on Liberia and the articles in its almost forty volumes represent a major contribution to scholarship on Liberia. Among the journal's editors have been Svend E. Holsoe, Mary Jo Sullivan, Edward Biggane, and D. Elwood Dunn, the current editor. The editorial address is: Department of Political Science, University of the South, Sewanee, TN 37375.

606 **Liberian Law Journal.**
Monrovia: Louis Arthur Grimes School of Law, University of Liberia, 1965- . biannual.
This law journal, edited at the University of Liberia's law school, is published in June and December each year and contains articles about Liberian law contributed by both Liberian and foreign authors.

607 **Liberia's rural radio plans.**
*New African*, (April 1979), p. 95.
Describes the plans at this time (1979) to use Liberia's rural radio in order to combat illiteracy.

608 **African newspapers in the Library of Congress.**
Compiled by John Pluge, Jr. Washington, DC: 1984. 2nd ed. 144p.
This resource can be found in the serial and government publications section of the Division of Research Services of the Library of Congress. It includes references to newspapers published in Liberia in the nineteenth century (p. 47-49). The publication is also available for sale from the United States Government Printing Office, Washington, DC.

609 **Liberian journalism, 1826-1980: a descriptive history.**
Momo Kpaka Rogers. PhD dissertation, School of Journalism, Southern Illinois University at Carbondale, Illinois, 1987. 326p.
This important study of print journalism (newspapers) in Liberia chronicles the history of Liberian newspapers. It also provides information on the social, cultural, economic, and political contexts within which the newspaper's editors and journalists functioned. It is based on extensive documentary evidence concerning 159 Liberian newspapers, magazines and other items published in Liberia between 1826 and 1980. The author is a former deputy minister in the Liberian government's Ministry of Information.

610 **The press in developing countries.**
Lloyd Ernest Sommerlad. Sydney, Australia: Sydney University Press, 1966. 189p.

This interesting study of journalism in developing countries touches on issues related to rural newspaper work in Liberia (p. 170-71). Wilbur Schramm writes in the foreword: 'In developing countries, newspapers are born in idealism and live in frustration. Many – most – of them die in frustration. In this book Lloyd Sommerlad puts flesh and blood on the statistics of newspapers foundings, newspapers difficulties, and newspaper failures in developing regions' (p. v).

611 **Problems of the Liberian Press.**
Edison Reginald Townsend. MA thesis, School of Social Sciences and Public Affairs, The American University, 1952. 114p.

Examines the difficulties and challenges of the Liberian press (print journalism) and refers to such issues as freedom of the press, economic problems, difficulties connected with technical equipment, and socio-political conditions affecting the press in Liberia. Townsend was Liberia's first cabinet-level information officer and was among government officials executed in 1980 in the wake of that year's *coup d'état*.

612 **Mass communication, culture and society in West Africa.**
Edited by Frank Okwu Ugboajah. Munich, New York, London, Oxford: Hans Zell; G. K. Saur for the World Association for Christian Communication, 1985. 329p. bibliog.

Articles in this volume which are of direct relevance to Liberia include: 'The media system of Liberia' by Jerome Zack Boikaii III (p. 36-43); and 'Broadcast music in Nigeria and Liberia: a comparative note' by Michael B. Read (p. 95-99). In addition, Barbara S. Monfils provides a bibliographical essay on mass media in West Africa (p. 285-308).

613 **University of Liberia Journal.**
Monrovia: University of Liberia Research Bureau/The Institute for Research, 1958- . irregular.

The semi-annual publication of the University of Liberia contains articles covering the humanities and the social and natural sciences. Most of the articles are written by Liberian or foreign Professors who have served at the University. Worlor Torpor, a philosophy Professor, was the editor of the publication during the 1970s.

614 **A model of mass communications and national development: a Liberian perspective.**
Abdulai Vandi. Washington, DC: University Press of America, 1979. 184p.

Studies the role of the mass media in modernization and education with particular reference to Liberia. A useful bibliography is also included.

615 **Making broadcasting useful, the African experience: the development of radio and television in Africa in the 1980s.**
Edited by George Wedell with the assistance of James Kangwana, Lawrence Lawler. Manchester, England: Manchester University Press, 1986. 306p.

This is a collection of papers on the development of broadcasting in sub-Saharan Africa in the 1980s. It developed from symposia on broadcasting organization and management in Africa sponsored by UNESCO and the European Institute for the Media, the UK Overseas Development Administration and the British Council. Divided into three parts and based on actual experiences, the volume covers a broad range of subjects including: 'Current issues' such as building programmes on limited budgets, and broadcasting and cultural change; 'Some country studies', among them Alhaji G. V. Kronah's 'The utilization of broadcasting for national development in Liberia' (p. 198-206); and 'An agenda for the future', which includes a list of practical recommendations by George Wedell and James Kangwana. Most of the authors have practical experience of broadcasting, and have been active in politics, administrative planning, training, or research.

616 **West Africa.**
London: West Africa, 1917- . weekly.

The longest running weekly news magazine dealing with sub-Saharan Africa, this publication now covers the entire continent. It reports on political and economic news, and provides regular articles on literature, as well as book reviews and interviews. It also publishes a 'writers' diary, excerpts from issues fifty and twenty-five years ago, and 'Dateline Africa' which consists of brief news items from each country in West Africa. Very valuable reports on the crisis Liberia faced in the 1930s, when the government was accused by the League of Nations of condoning a form of forced labour, can be found within its pages. Issues of a more contemporary nature which the magazine has covered include the 1980 military *coup d'état* and the turbulent years of the 1980s which culminated in the civil war which began on 24 December 1989 and as yet remains unresolved (1994).

# Encyclopaedias and Reference Works

617 **International guide to African studies research.**
Compiled by Philip Baker. New York: G. K. Saur; London: Hans Zell
Publishers, 1987. 264p.

Presented in English and French, this guide provides an international forum for
Africanists of all countries. It contains more than 1,100 numbered entries organized by
country. Within each country the entries are arranged alphabetically by name, or
organization. Liberia is featured on page 91, and includes information on the Liberian
Institute for Biomedical Research, the Tubman Centre for African Culture, the
University of Liberia's African Studies Program and the Medical School, and the West
African Rice Development Association (WARDA) which once had its headquarters in
Monrovia.

618 **African boundaries: a legal and diplomatic encyclopaedia.**
Ian Brownlie, with the assistance of Ian R. Burns, C. Hurst (et al.).
London: University of California Press for the Royal Institute of
International Affairs, 1979. 1,355p.

This 'systematic study of African boundaries' presented as a reference work focuses on
the current legal status of boundaries excluding those of a maritime nature. As far as
possible the text reports positions as they stood at the close of 1977. The three areas of
particular interest to Liberia are: Ivory Coast/Liberia (p. 358-78); Liberia-Sierra Leone
(p. 379-405); and Guinea-Liberia (p. 304-09). Each of these subsections contains
chapters on 'General provenance'; 'Alignment'; and 'Evidence' with maps and
chronological tables of documents. A bibliography ends each subsection, and there is a
general index at the end of the study.

**619 The Liberian Year-book, 1956.**
Edited by Henry B. Cole.    Monrovia, Liberia: Consolidated
Publications, 1957.

This compilation contains dated but interesting information on the press, broadcasting, business and industry, and other basic facts about Liberia in the mid-1950s. There is also a section containing biographies of leading citizens.

**620 The Liberian Year-book for 1962.**
Edited by Henry B. Cole.    Monrovia, Liberia, 1962. 279p. illus.

This is the second edition of a comprehensive handbook (erratic in publication) which first appeared in 1957. The twenty-one chapters present factual information about all matters relating to Liberia – the land and the people, government and administration, economic, social, political, and cultural life. Lists of names and addresses of officials, business firms, and institutions of various kinds are also included. Of related interest is the *Handbook and Directory of Liberia*, which was published for the Chamber of Commerce in Monrovia by the Consolidated Publications Company in 1963 (132p.).

**621 Guide to research and reference works on sub-Saharan Africa.**
Edited by Peter Duignan, compiled by Helen F. Conover, Peter Duignan,
with the assistance of Evelyn Boyce, Lisolette Hoffman, Karen Fung.
Stanford, California: Hoover Institution Press, Stanford University, 1971.
1,102p. (Hoover Institution Bibliographical Series, XLVI).

Describes 'African library and archival materials important in reference, research, and teaching'. The volume's 3,127 items provide an excellent reference bibliography for the entire field of African studies up to 1970. Moreover, most entries are annotated. Part one is a 'Guide to research organizations, libraries and archives and the booktrade' (p. 1-87); part two has 'Bibliographies for Africa in general' (p. 91-152); part three is a 'Subject guide in general' (p. 155-400); and part four provides an 'Area guide (by former colonial power, region, and country)' (p. 403-941). All references are indexed by author, title, subject and geographical location. Material specifically on Liberia appears in items 459-466, and on p. 52.

**622 Historical dictionary of Liberia.**
D. Elwood Dunn, Svend E. Holsoe.    Metuchen, New Jersey: Scarecrow
Press, 1985. 304p.

Provides short dictionary-style entries on major historical events, important places, leading figures, and significant aspects of the culture, religion, and political economy of Liberia. The volume covers the different populations of the country and members of the leadership groups, and provides biographical summaries of important historical figures drawn from all spheres of Liberian life including: traditional rulers, colonizers, repatriate leaders, the clergy, educators, politicians, professionals and the military. With a useful chronology and an extensive general bibliography, the work also has an index, and is valuable as a reference for the researcher and the general reader.

623 **Political leaders of contemporary Africa south of the Sahara: a bibliographical dictionary.**
Edited by Harvey Glickman.   Westport, Connecticut; London: Greenwood Press, 1992. 392p.

This selective biographical dictionary of fifty-three post-1945 political leaders in sub-Saharan Africa assesses how these figures have helped shape events in the continent and what political impact they have had on individual countries and regions. The profiles are arranged alphabetically and are accompanied by short bibliographies of works by, and about, the leaders. Liberians profiled are 'Samuel Kanyon Doe' by C. William Allen (p. 68-74) and 'William Vacanarat Shadrach Tubman' by D. Elwood Dunn (p. 291-96).

624 **African states and rulers: an encyclopedia of native, colonial and independent states and rulers past and present.**
John Stewart Jefferson.   North Carolina: McFarland, 1989. 395p.

The stated purpose of this work is 'to tell succinctly the political story of the Dark Continent, making it clear what happened in each country'. African history is divided into native, colonial and independent phases with entries listed alphabetically by country. An index of 'rulers' is also provided. The entry relating to Liberia is found on p. 159-60 along with cross references.

625 **Africa contemporary record: annual survey and records.**
Edited by Colin Legum.   London: Rex Collings, 1969-79. New York, London: Africana Publishing, 1979- . annual.

This publication provides a very useful survey and selections of important documents. Each volume features a series of essays on current issues (political developments, social affairs, foreign relations etc.), country-by-country reviews of events, and includes statistical information and addresses. Indexes of documents and subjects are also provided.

626 **Africa south of the Sahara: index to periodical literature.**
Boston, Massachusetts: G. K. Hall, 1971, 1982; Washington, DC: Library of Congress, African Section, African and Middle Eastern Division, 1985- . irregular.

This is an on-going publication that began as the *Index to Periodical Literature, 1900-1970* (Boston, Massachusetts, G. K. Hall, 1971, 3 vols.). *The Second Supplement* (Boston, Massachusetts: G. K. Hall, 1982, 3 vols.) covered periodical literature from June 1972-December 1976. *The Third Supplement*, (Washington, DC: Library of Congress African Section, 1985) includes citations to African periodicals published in 1977 arranged in six subject categories and subdivided by country. Also helpful is *US Imprints on Sub-Saharan Africa: A Guide to Publications Catalogued at the Library of Congress* (Washington, DC: Library of Congress, African Section, 1985- . annual), compiled under the direction of Joanne M. Zellers.

627 **Handbook to the modern world.**
Edited by Sean Moroney. New York: Facts on Files Series, 1989.
2 vols.

The first volume of this work contains basic information on each country of the world, listed in alphabetical order, whilst the entries in volume two are grouped under political affairs, economic affairs, and social affairs (the entry for Liberia begins on page 279).

628 **Black Africa, a comparative handbook.**
Donald George Morrison, Robert Cameron Mitchell, John Naber Paden.
New York: Irvington Publishers, 1989. 716p.

First published in 1972, this useful handbook provides comparative data on a wide range of topics. Black Africa is defined as those parts of sub-Saharan Africa which are governed by black Africans. The stated intention of the study is to provide reliable information in order to facilitate comparative political, economic and social analysis and inquiry, and hence contribute to 'the development of theory and empirically verified generalization.' The current edition was developed from an African National Integration Project at the Massachusetts Institute of Technology, the purpose of which was to investigate problems of conflict, national integration, social mobilization and political change. Part one, presents a comparative profile which includes 'over 150 tables containing nearly 300 indicators for the measurement of concepts and the testing of theory' (p. xxxii). Part two offers country profiles and provides information about each country's ethnic, linguistic, urban, and political situation in the period of political independence. The section of part two which covers Liberia (p. 523-30) offers basic information, and details of ethnic, language, urban, and political patterns, national integration and stability. There is a useful selected bibliography.

629 **Liberia Annual Review.**
Edited by Bobby Naidoo. Monrovia: Consolidated Publications, 1963.
[irregular] 360p.

Included in this rather comprehensive review are basic facts, brief reports on various government activities, a 'who's who' in Liberia, a list of commercial firms, and a list of diplomatic missions to Liberia.

630 **The Cambridge encyclopaedia of Africa.**
Edited by Roland Oliver, Michael Crowder. Cambridge, England; New
York: Cambridge University Press, 1981. 492p. 46 maps. bibliog.

This illustrated reference volume containing work by ninety-nine contributors surveys all major aspects of Africa. The chapter titles include 'The African continent' (physical environment and peoples); 'The African past'; 'Contemporary Africa'; and 'Africa and the world'. Liberia (p. 239) is well described by David Williams.

631 **The United States in Africa: a historical dictionary.**
David Shavit. New York: Greenwood Press, 1989. 320p.

This is a reference work which 'provides in one alphabetical format a resource on more than 700 people, organizations, and events that have affected the relations between the United States and Africa from the 1600s to the present.' Liberia figures prominently in this compilation.

# Bibliographies

632 **Black African literature in English since 1952.**
Barbara Abrash, with an introduction by John F. Povey. New York: Johnson Reprint Corporation, 1967. 92p.

A bibliography containing books and articles concerned with African literary history and criticism as well as anthologies and individual works by several African writers. Included are the works of Roland T. Dempster and Bai T. Moore of Liberia.

633 **A world bibliography of African bibliographies.**
Compiled by Theodore Besterman, revised and updated by J. D. Pearson. Oxford: Blackwell; Totowa, New Jersey: Rowman & Littlefield, 1975. 4th ed. 241 columns.

The current edition of this work contains 1,634 unannotated entries on African items published prior to 1973. The listing for Liberia (column 123) is organized by subject.

634 **Africa bibliography 1992. Works on Africa in 1992.**
Compiled by Christopher H. Allen (University of Edinburgh) with the assistance of Katherine Allen in association with the International African Institute, London. Edinburgh: Edinburgh University Press. 430p. annual.

The fourth edition of this major annual bibliography records publications on Africa in the areas of the social sciences, environmental sciences, humanities and the arts. The compilation, which has been annually updated since 1983, is arranged regionally and by country, with a preliminary section for the continent as a whole. Featured are three types of publication – periodical articles, books, and essays in edited volumes or chapters from books. Author and subject indexes provide easy access to the material. The Liberia section, under the West Africa heading, is on pages 158-60.

635 **African women: a general bibliography, 1976-1985.**
Compiled by Davis A. Bullwinkle. New York: Greenwood Press, 1989.
335p.

Heralded as the first of a three-volume African Special Bibliographical Series, this volume includes some citations which are not identified by a region or nation in Africa. The author claims to have 'made a conscientious effort to cover African women in all facets of their world including such diverse subject areas as sexual mutilation, nutrition, abortion, and literature'. Forthcoming second and third volumes will be entitled respectively: *Women of Northern, Western and Central Africa: a bibliography, 1976-1985*; and *Women in Eastern and Southern Africa: a bibliography, 1976-1985*.

636 **Africa south of the Sahara: a selected, annotated list of writings.**
Compiled by Helen F. Conover. Washington, DC: General Reference
& Bibliography Division, Reference Department Library of Congress,
1963. 345p.

The compiler provides excellent annotations and indexes for 2,173 items covering all aspects of sub-Saharan Africa. The entries are arranged in topical sections and by country. The Liberia section (p. 113-18) covers entries 651-680 and contains thirty-two important references. See also the compiler's earlier *Liberia: a selected list of references* (Washington, DC: Library of Congress, 1942. 13p.).

637 **Annotated bibliography of materials available in the documentation
center, bureau of planning, ministry of education.**
Compiled by Leo Eastman. Monrovia: Government of Liberia, 1973.
46p.

A collection of some 208 titles including material from government ministries and agencies, and sources concerning education emanating from UNESCO, various UN agencies, as well as other organizations.

638 **Selected bibliography on rural Liberia.**
Richard Melvin Fulton. *Rural Africana*, no. 15 (1971), p. 123-41.
This is a brief compilation of books, theses, and bibliographies on rural Liberia.

639 **Liberia under the Tolbert era: a guide.**
Compiled by Beverly Ann Gray, Angel Batiste. Washington, DC:
Library of Congress, 1983. 78p. (Maktabe Africana Series).

This bibliography is a compilation of selected Liberian government documents, as well as books, pamphlets, periodical articles, and dissertations about the country during the administration of President William R. Tolbert, Jr. (from July 1971 to April 1980). Unfortunately, this list includes only the holdings of the Library of Congress.

# Bibliographies

640 **A bibliography of primary sources for nineteenth century tropical Africa as recorded by explorers, missionaries, traders, travelers, administrators, military men, adventurers, and others.**
Compiled by Robert L. Hess, Dalvan M. Coger. Pala Alto, California: Hoover Institution Press, Stanford University, 1973. 800p.

More than 7,000 primary sources are listed in this bibliography and particular emphasis is placed on works which reveal what Africa was like on the eve of European partition and during the early colonial era. The volume is organized by geographical region and an author index is included. Presented in very rough form with considerable ink markings in the text, it first appeared in 1971.

641 **A bibliography of Liberian government documents.**
Svend E. Holsoe. *African Studies Bulletin*, vol. 11, no. 1 (April 1968), p. 39-63; vol. 11, no. 2 (Sept. 1968), p. 149-94.

This bibliography represents the first known attempt to provide a comprehensive listing of various types of printed and duplicated Liberian government documents. Arrangement is by subject and by government agency. The compiler, a professor of anthropology at the University of Delaware, has a draft update (to the early 1980s) bibliography of Liberian government documents that has not been published.

642 **A bibliography on Liberia, part one: books.**
Svend E. Holsoe. Liberian Studies Association in America, 1971. 125p.
(Liberian Studies Research Working Paper, no. 1).

Entries are listed alphabetically and the index cites materials by subject and provides names of co-authors and individuals who have written introductions or forewords to the works. Also available are *A bibliography on Liberia, part two: publications concerning colonization* (Liberian Studies Research Working Paper, no. 3, 1971. 63p.) which is divided into three sections which include works published by the American Colonization Society, general published material on African colonization and the colonization of specific states. Each section is arranged alphabetically and an index is also included. The third publication entitled *A bibliography on Liberia, part three: articles* (Liberian Studies Research Working Paper, no. 5, 1976. 169p) contains references to materials which refer primarily to Liberia.

643 **A bibliography of Liberian languages.**
Frances Ingemann. *Anthropological Linguistics*, vol. 20, no. 2 (Feb. 1978), p. 64-76.

This brief, but interesting, bibliographical essay is divided into sections which correspond to the various ethnic groupings of Liberia. Following a section on general works, items are listed respectively under the following groups: Mel (Southern West Atlantic), Mande, Kruan, and Liberian English (a lingua franca that originates from the speech patterns of settler-Liberians) with each having appropriate sub-groups.

644 **Cumulative bibliography of African studies.**
International African Institute Library. London: G. K. Hall, 1973.
3 vols.

This reference work began as a quarterly bibliography of current books and articles which was published in the journal *Africa* from 1929 to 1970, and thereafter as a separate bulletin entitled *International African Bibliography*. The initial emphasis was on ethnography and languages, though it was later expanded to include other areas of African studies. The study features both an author and a classified catalogue. The author catalogue has three sections; book reviews, abstracts, and the library holding of the International African Institute Library (collection of books, pamphlets, and census reports). In the classified catalogue subject headings are arranged alphabetically in geographical sections. Liberia is featured in vol. two (p. 421-31).

645 **The urban informal sector in Africa in retrospect and prospect: an annotated bibliography.**
Washington, DC: International Labour Office. 1991. 86p.
This study is concerned with the urban poor and includes 200 recent titles in English and French, covering: regional variations; training; credit; women; policies and the institutional environment; links between the formal and informal sectors; as well as intervention by aid organizations.

646 **The sources of the literature of Liberian history: part one.**
Abeodu Bowen Jones (assisted by Svend E. Holsoe). *The Liberian Historical Review*, vol. 2, no. 1 (1965), p. 37-38.
Contains a list of library sources, both Liberian and foreign, which are useful for the study of Liberian history.

647 **A bibliography of books and articles on Liberia as edited in German speaking countries since 1960.**
Compiled by Robert Kappel, Werner Korte. Bremen, Germany: Liberia Working Group, 1989. 53p. (Paper no. 3).
Supplementing Svend Holsoe's three-volume *Bibliography on Liberia* (q.v.), this is a useful compilation of studies on Liberia produced in Germany, Lichtenstein and Switzerland. The volume includes books, statistical studies, doctoral theses and articles covering a wide-range of topics. The final nine unnumbered pages contain a helpful index of authors and subjects.

648 **A bibliography of the Malaguetta Coast (actual Liberia) until 1848.**
Andreas Massing. *University of Liberia Journal*, vol. 13, no. 2 (July 1971), p. 32-37.
The bibliography mainly lists primary sources and is divided into a Portuguese period, a Dutch period, and the period from 1700-1848. The work also includes selected secondary materials.

649 **Missions and education in Liberia: a check list of annotated writings (1824-1977) on Western education in Liberia with emphasis on its mission origins.**
Fawani Nguma. PhD Thesis, University of Missouri-Kansas City, 1979 (in two parts). 583p.
An annotated bibliography of writings relating to the first one hundred and fifty years of Western education in Liberia. The work contains more than a thousand entries and is arranged topically and chronologically. An introduction to the check list provides an

overview of modern education in Liberia highlighting its Western content. Part I is entitled 'Support of education in Liberia from foreign sources, 1824-1987'; part II, 'The state of education in Liberia; some historical and present aspects 1832-1977'; and part III, 'Reference books (biographies and directories).'

650  **Research at Cuttington University College, 1952-1983.**
Compiled by Emmanuel Nyamadi.  Bong County, Liberia: Cuttington University College, 1984. [n.p.].

This is an annotated bibliography of theses and senior graduate papers presented at Cuttington from 1952 to 1983.

651  **Linguistics and Liberian languages in the 1970s and 1980s: a bibliography.**
John Victor Singler.  *Liberian Studies Journal*, vol. 15, no. 1 (1990), p. 108-26.

Following a brief historical overview of the languages of Liberia and references to works on Liberian languages, this bibliography of articles and books concentrates on three topics: Liberia's Niger-Congo languages; Liberian English; and language use in Liberia. The Niger-Congo family is presented as Mende, West Atlantic, and Kru; and Liberian English is divided into Liberian Standard English, Kru Pidgin English and Liberian Interior English. The author makes the point that scholarly interest in Liberian languages has been limited to non-Liberians (p. 112).

652  **A general bibliography of Liberia.**
Marvin D. Solomon, Warren L. d'Azevedo.  Evanston, Illinois: Northwestern University Press, 1962. (Northwestern Working Paper, no. 10).

This comprehensive bibliography contains works by both Liberian and foreign writers dating from the earliest times to 1962. The bibliography lists books, pamphlets, articles, speeches, maps, government documents and several other types of publication. There are over 2,000 entries, including references to periodicals.

653  **African art: a bibliographic guide.**
Compiled by Janet L. Stanley.  New York, London: Africana, 1985. 55p. (Smithsonian Institution Libraries Research Guide, no. 4).

This critical guide to the 'best books' on the subject, provides informative annotations for each item. The 167 entries are arranged in nine categories: 'Periodicals'; 'Bibliographies and reference books'; 'General surveys'; 'Regional studies'; 'African crafts and utilitarian arts'; 'Architecture'; 'Rock art, stone sculpture and ancient terracottas'; 'Contemporary African art and tourist art'; and 'African art market and collecting African art'. The compiler is a Librarian at the National Museum of African Art, Smithsonian Institution, Washington, DC.

654 **A bibliography of the Vai language and script.**
Gail B. Stewart, P. E. H. Hair. *Journal of West African Languages*,
vol. 7, no. 2 (1969), p. 109-24.

This is perhaps the most exhaustive, partially annotated, bibliography on the Vai language and script currently available. Though the historical date for the invention of the script is given as 1830 and its discovery by Europe as about 1850, Stewart and Hair point out that 'the earliest certain reference in historical sources to the Vai language is in an account of the Cape Mount area published in 1668 but probably written before 1650' (p. 109). Following a very useful introduction, the bibliography, which consists of some thirteen pages, is arranged chronologically by date of publication. However, as the compilers state 'writings of Vai ethnography containing occasional terms in Vai are not included. Titles are given in full only for items wholly in or on Vai, or rare' (p. 111).

655 **An annotated bibliography of Liberian forestry and botany, 1849-1964.**
J. V. Thirgood.   Monrovia: College of Agriculture & Forestry,
University of Liberia, 1964.

Contains works by both Liberian and foreign writers, the latter being more numerous.

656 **A bibliography of the Negro in Africa and America.**
Compiled by Monroe Nathan Work.   New York: Argosy-Antiquarian,
1965. 697p.

This work was first published in 1928 and reprinted in 1965. It includes sections dealing with early African civilizations, slavery and the slave trade, and independent governments in Africa, among them Abyssinia and Liberia. Listed on pages 121-24 are books, articles and other items on Liberia.

# Indexes

There follow three separate indexes: authors (personal and corporate); titles; and subjects. Title entries are italicized and refer either to the main titles, or to other works cited in the annotations. The numbers refer to bibliographical entry rather than page numbers. Individual index entries are arranged in alphabetical sequence.

## Index of Authors

177

# Index of Titles

# L

193

195

# Index of Subjects

197

# Map of Liberia

This map shows the more important towns and other features.

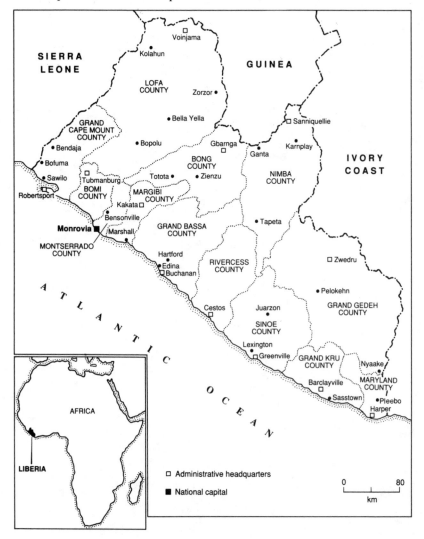